"I've read Carollo's memoir and
tion, moved by its profundity, anc
Carollo has created an enviable leg

- Malcolm Whyte, author, poet

"In *The Unknown Composer*, John A. Carollo tells his life story with honesty and dignity, showing us how he found his way from feeling lost to 'transfiguring' himself through music. 'Music wasn't entering me, it was awakening within me.' His writing is clear and genuine, making readers actually 'feel the empowerment of music' and personal growth. This book is a touching reminder of how influential our spirits are and how crucial it is to follow our true calling."

- Sonja Koch, author of *Bookends of Life*

"As performers, we're trained to seek the stage. John's memoir is a striking counterpoint. A life devoted to composition without the need for recognition, finding meaning in the act itself."

- Hugh Sung, pianist, former Director of Instrumental Accompaniment and Student Recitals at Curtis Institute of Music

"A celebration of creativity, Carollo's memoir is an invitation to explore and discover artistic expression and composition, to take a risk, to see where it leads. There is an element of excitement in the not knowing, in following one's creative instincts, in music. 'Without the arts, the soul goes silent.' Punctuated throughout with poetry and music, *The Unknown Composer* is an inspirational read!"

- Betty R. Wall, author of *No Way Out* and *All That This House Has To Offer*

# THE UNKNOWN COMPOSER

A Memoir:
From Innocence to Awareness,
From Mystery to Clarity

JOHN A. CAROLLO

*atmosphere press*

Published by Atmosphere Press

Cover design by Felipe Betim



Atmospherepress.com

For David
My great love,
and to every artist who composes in silence—
unheard, but never unseen by the soul that seeks.

# PREFACE

This memoir is an invitation to journey through the intertwined paths of sound and silence, memory and imagination, loss and renewal. It tells the story of a life devoted to creative expression from an essential need to give voice to the inner world.

Within these pages, you will encounter a narrative of a composer and poet; reflections on identity, belonging, and the search for meaning. The musical works referenced are markers of transformation and discovery—each one is a step toward deeper knowing.

It is my hope that readers will find resonance in these stories—whether through shared experience or the stirring of new questions—and that they offer a space to come to the table of contemplation, to reflect on the mysteries of creativity and the quiet power of art to endure beyond its maker.

*To write, to compose, to create is to engage in a dialogue with eternity.*

# TABLE OF CONTENTS

*"A listen through my entire catalogue will tell you everything.*
*It is my diary in sound."*

– John A. Carollo

# INTRODUCTION
## A Life in Myth, Silence, and Sound

*Music unheard is more valuable than music heard, for in silence it retains its full potential—uncontaminated, unclaimed.*

*Performers seldom seek out new works unless well-compensated. Meanwhile, artists are expected to bring forth their creations on their own, often without financial support.*

*I am the unknown composer; I prefer it this way.*

## THE UNKNOWN COMPOSER

*No one is left*
*to write an account of my life.*

*All have perished*
*silently*
*into that good night.*

*The fear of the unknown*
*haunts me.*

*My life has been*
*a daily unfolding*
*of the unknown—*
*unknown music,*

*unknown beginnings,*
*unknown self.*

*The mystery that is Giovanni Baudino*
*aka John A. Carollo,*
*cannot be known.*

*Indescribable.*
*Likewise, my music.*

*With Bill's death,*
*life has been a journey*
*of self-discovery.*

*Perhaps the unknown*
*will become known,*
*slowly,*
*one note at a time.*

Remaining a mystery serves my artistic aims. It is also a comfort to walk down any street without being recognized. There are no paparazzi, no limelight, no demands to explain the current work, the next work, or the older works—just a blissful existence, composing until death do us part.

Music has been my constant companion—the silent witness to every joy and sorrow, every moment of longing or fulfillment. In the quiet hours, when others might seek solace in conversation or touch, I have always turned to sonic vibrations. Where words have failed me, music has remained faithful.

Much like mythological figures shaped by fate, my life has been a tapestry of complex conditions.

I was placed in an institute for infants. That was the beginning.

Within months, I was transferred to the nunnery section of a grand basilica—Superga—perched above Torino, where I spent the first four and a half years of my life.

A child of silence, cradled between heaven and stone.

Eventually, I boarded a plane with an escort and flew to New York City, then on to Pittsburgh, where I was met by my adoptive parents, Tony and Mary Carollo. They drove me to Oil City, Pennsylvania, where I was to begin again. They were second-generation Italians who spoke a dialect I didn't understand. I cried the entire way until we stopped at a restaurant.

It was enough, just barely, to quiet my cries.

Mary told me that the warmth of the soup and the unfamiliar tang of American bread put a smile on my face. I must have sensed comfort was fleeting, but at that moment, it was enough.

*Believing* I was an orphan—and, later, believing I was abandoned—became a persistent wound. That pain of rejection is woven into my personality. It's there in my music, and in the fabric of a thirty-seven-and-a-half-year love affair with an older man, thirty years my senior.

My music, at times, aches with that longing—a subtle mourning for what was lost or never found. The melodies are not always sad, but they carry a searching quality, a yearning for connection that I struggled to find elsewhere.

It led to an isolated existence where internal dialogues took precedence over external ones, making friendships awkward. I turned this isolation into my dearest companion. In solitude, I learned to listen to the shifting patterns of my thoughts, to the sounds of the world outside my window, to the music that would eventually rise out of that silence. Loneliness became a kind of teacher, shaping my inner landscape.

At thirty-two, I began composing music—an obsession

that never let go.

This memoir seeks to elucidate that journey—to document my life in parallel with my musical oeuvre, a catalogue of several hundred works—and to tell my story as only I can. Many of the players are gone. They can no longer serve as eyewitnesses. They cannot fill in the gaps in memory.

I am left to stitch together fragments—some clear, some blurred by time and longing. Memory is a fragile thread, but it is all I have.

So, how do you write a self when the supporting cast has vanished?

I will do my best to speak from a subjective truth. Few remain to tell the story of a child separated from his birth mother, raised by adoptive parents who neither played instruments nor understood music, who left home at twenty-one and moved to San Diego in 1976—falling in love within two months with a tall, handsome psychiatrist named Bill.

Bill became my mentor, critic and beloved—until his death in 2014, just three months after our marriage was finally sanctified. Those three months were strange and precious gifts. After decades of secrecy, to have our bond named and witnessed—even briefly—felt like a benediction. Loss came swiftly on its heels, but for a moment, I was seen.

We could not raise a family. Society would not accept our love. Would I live my older years without the rituals that comfort others? No birthday celebrations, no wine country trips, no shared mourning, no children or grandchildren to visit me in old age?

Why do I write music? Because I know no other way to speak my truth. When I sit at the keyboard, I become both more myself and somehow beyond myself. Each note is a word I cannot say aloud, each phrase a confession I would never dare share otherwise.

From simple piano sketches to abstract sonic explorations,

my music traces a life lived in reflection, passion, and wonder. I render these works in Finale—a professional music notation software—using a MIDI keyboard (a controller for entering notes, not a sound-producing instrument) and a wide monitor. I compose daily, not for accolades or fame, but to please the inner child who refuses to grow up.

Several of the part titles in this memoir share names with musical works I have composed. This is intentional. Just as my music reflects the emotional and spiritual landscapes of my life, the structure of this book echoes those creative landmarks. Each part marks a phase of becoming and a body of work that arose from that season of inner growth.

I now feel free, content, and ready to share this life story—hopeful it might resonate with someone suffering in silence.

What follows is a personal account of the unknown composer, John A. Carollo, born Giovanni Baudino.

If you too have lived in silence—if you have wondered whether your story matters—know that you are not alone. The unknown can be daunting, but it also holds the possibility of beauty. My hope is that in these pages, and in these notes, you might find comfort, curiosity, or simply the courage to keep listening.

From the music that carries my innermost truths, we now turn to the silence that shaped me—the early years cloaked in mystery and absence. This is where my journey begins: in the quiet shadows of Torino, beneath the gaze of a grand basilica, where a child unknown waited to be found.

# PART I

## Origins

# CHAPTER 1

## The Birth of Silence: Origins and the Flight into Mystery

*I entered the world as a mystery wrapped in silence.*

I was born Giovanni Baudino on November 4, 1954, in Torino, Italy. Nine days later, I was placed in an institute for infants. The silence of those early days settled deep in my bones. It was not a memory of an event, but of a feeling—of being unseen, unknown.

A few months later, I was transferred to the Basilica di Superga, a vast Baroque structure perched above Torino, where the nuns took me in. Their habits whispered as they passed. I lived there for over four years, a child of silence, gazing out over a city that did not know me. Somewhere between God and sky, my identity dissolved. I became invisible—a vessel of waiting.

I have no memory of the nunnery. No memory of my mother's face, her touch, or the long journey that brought me to a foreign land. Bill, my husband of thirty-seven-and-a-half years and a psychiatrist, once told me this absence of memory was a sign of childhood depression. My adoptive mother, Mary, told me later in life that I used to complain, shortly after arriving in Oil City, about a nun who kept "pinching me."

I want to believe the caretakers at the nunnery were kind. That they met my needs. That I was hugged, loved, wanted—receiving what young children need for good brain development and emotional well-being.

*Basilica di Superga, perched above Torino. My childhood home for over four years—a place of silence, separation, and mystery.*

Yet, the silence remains, an ache just under the surface.

In 2022—sixty-seven years after my birth—my search for the truth finally began. I received extraordinary news from an Italian genealogist who had been researching my ancestry. After combing through Turin's archives, she discovered that my birth mother, Rosanna Baudino, had died on December 18, 2000.

My adoptive parents had shared what little they had been told. The genealogist wrote that Rosanna was born on April 18, 1933, in Torino. Later in life, she moved to Bosconero, a small town just north of the city. At the time of my birth, she was working as a waitress. Her mother was Elisa Meaglia. Her father, Matteo, had died before I was born. The town hall in Bosconero could even identify her grave, and I was told there might be a photo on the tombstone.

My birth father, however, remains a mystery—a shadow with no name. Was he musical? Was he kind to Rosanna? Was he a phantom, much like the adoptive father I would come to know?

The genealogist uncovered something else—a joyous surprise: I had two half-siblings living in Bosconero. Rosanna married sometime after giving birth to me. The investigator wrote to them, requesting permission to release their names. When they consented, I waited two months before reaching out. I wanted to be sure I got it right, to feel completely ready—even though my newfound family seemed to have made little effort to find me. That thought had haunted me for decades.

Eventually, I emailed my half-brother, Lorenzo, and my half-sister, Josephine, introducing myself and attaching a recent photo. I found Lorenzo's Facebook page and sent a friend request, which he accepted right away. Writing those first messages was one of the most difficult things I've ever done. How do you introduce yourself to family you've never met? I agonized over every word, wanting to sound open but not desperate, cautious but not cold. I attached my photo, wondering if they'd spot any resemblance—any sign that I belonged.

Since then, Lorenzo and I have chatted every day, getting to know each other with a warmth that feels both natural and surreal. Through him, I learned my birth father had been a military police officer, though no further details ever surfaced. Lorenzo was thrilled I'd found him—welcoming, generous, and full of stories I never imagined I'd hear.

Discovering a brother in adulthood is almost surreal, like piecing together stories from opposite ends of a life neither of us lived together. With each exchange, I felt the comfort of recognition—the tentative stitching together of a family story I'd always longed for, even if never acknowledged consciously.

When Josephine (Giusy) responded, it was with a gentle reserve. We compared photos, searching for echoes of ourselves in each other's faces. I found myself studying their features, their gestures, hoping to glimpse a reflection of myself—proof that I was not an orphan in the world, but tethered by blood and history to something larger.

There was both joy and grief in the connection—a sense of what had been lost, but also what could still be found. In their warmth, I discovered something I hadn't known I was missing: the possibility of belonging.

For the past two and a half years, Giusy has shared many revealing aspects about Rosanna, our common mother. She was poor, living in an old, dilapidated house that someone else owned. The landlord, full of compassion, let her and her husband stay there rent-free, as Rosanna was destitute and struggling. Her husband—Lorenzo's and Giusy's father—was an alcoholic, and the instability of their life eventually led Rosanna to divorce him.

This news brought me sadness and grief. I imagined her loneliness, her quiet suffering, and the daily weight of poverty pressing down on her spirit. It pained me to realize that, in her most vulnerable years, her only support system was Giusy and Lorenzo—her own children—doing what they could to lift her from those difficult circumstances.

I could have been there for my sister, who dropped out of grade school to care for the woman who bore me. I might have shared her burden, lightened her sorrow.

Giusy once messaged me: "Your mum would have been happy and maybe (if you had found her) ... The pain she felt every day ... would have helped her ... She didn't know how to read and write ... Only her signature ... And I did the shopping ... With money ... she couldn't ... Go shopping ... I'll tell you many things verbally ... When the war began in 1939, Rosanna was six years old. Schools were closed.

No one got an education."

I cried a river of tears. My sister became the mother, and my mother, the daughter.

Rosanna's life seemed marked by hardship, yet she endured. And from that endurance came three children—separated by fate, yet bound by blood and memory. Knowing this part of her story filled in a silence I had long carried, but it also left me aching for the mother I never truly knew.

Years before, I had already begun my own lonely search. I had written to Catholic Charities in Erie, Pennsylvania, reviewed the few documents my adoptive parents had kept, and visited the Provincial Institute for Infants, where I was placed shortly after Rosanna had given me the sacred gift of life.

I learned that I was born at Ospedale Sant'Anna Hospital in Torino and baptized on November 12, 1954, at the Patrocinio di San Giuseppe. My mother had breastfed me after admission to La nuova sede dell'Istituto Provinciale per l'Infanzia (IPAI) facility. She worked as a domestic.

Rosanna had been told to either bring me home or give me up for adoption. Living with her elderly mother and unable to support me, she made the heartbreaking decision to surrender me.

Despite these details, I carry many questions. Many doubts. A reservoir of heartbreak for what could have been, and what was denied.

Bill warned me about the search I was about to begin. He told me it might be like opening Pandora's box—a flood of emotions and truths that, once unleashed, could never be contained again. I wasn't sure I was ready for what might come. But the need to know, to break the silence, was stronger than my fear.

Sometimes, the deepest wounds carry the loudest call for healing.

There's a peculiar kind of anticipation that comes with waiting for news about your own origin—a mix of dread and hope that sits in the pit of your stomach. When the genealogist's email finally arrived, I hesitated before opening it. I stared at the subject line, heart thrumming in my chest, as if the answer inside could somehow rewrite the past.

Seeing my mother's name in black and white, the details of her life stripped down to dates and places, was both exhilarating and devastating. Each fact—her birth in Torino, her death in Bosconero, the name of her mother and father—felt like a small rescue from oblivion.

I wish I could say that each new discovery brought relief or a sense of closure, but it didn't. More often, it opened into new questions—deeper doubts.

In 2007, 23andMe, the personal genomics and biotechnology company offering direct-to-consumer DNA testing, came online. "This is it," I said to myself. Now an Italian family member might find me, or I might find them! I created a profile using my Italian birth name and uploaded the photo that once appeared on my Italian passport.

Years passed with no success. Hoping for a different outcome, I tried Ancestry.com, then MyHeritage.com. Still, nothing. Maybe my family isn't curious, I thought. Or maybe they're simply not tech-savvy. Either way, the silence was deafening.

After the *60 Minutes* story *The Vatican's Orphans* aired on October 13, 2024, I learned even more. With help from John Campitelli—an advocate for Italian adoptees who managed a Facebook group and was featured in the book that inspired the broadcast—I discovered I had been reduced to a case number and sold by the Catholic Church to a deeply religious Italian-American couple in Oil City, Pennsylvania.

I wept for ten minutes. Uncontrollably.

John had responded to my Facebook inquiry with four images and no words (see Appendix B). One showed the Children's Manifest for Flight ICEM-12992, including case numbers. Another was a photo of the airplane, a Dutch aircraft with Royal Dutch Airlines. A third was a typed index card with my adoptive parents' contact information. The last was a Declaration Form identifying the crew members and the captain, who was the legal guardian for the children on board.

My name, Giovanni Baudino, appeared among the eight children flown to the United States. I was case number 21027.

When I saw my name on the flight manifest, I felt a strange surge of pride and shame. There I was—named, numbered, and sent away. A child catalogued for export.

John told me the author's cousin had been on the same flight.

According to *The Price of Children: Stolen Lives in a Land Without Choice* by Maria Laurino, between 1950 and 1970, the Vatican and the American Catholic Church conspired to send nearly four thousand Italian children to the U.S. for adoption into "good" Catholic homes. Masquerading as a service for orphaned children, the program was in truth an effort to address the stigma of unwed motherhood. Mothers were shamed, misled, and coerced. Some were told their babies had died. Others signed documents they could not read.

Knowing I was one of those children still shakes me. For years, my own investigations led me to believe I had a mother, Rosanna, but I could never be certain. I wanted it to be true. No one ever gave me a photograph of her, or a copy of her birth certificate.

That uncertainty haunted me until just two and a half years ago, when I was sixty-seven years old. The investigator

I had hired in San Francisco sent me copies of my birth mother's birth and death certificates—documents finally unearthed by a professional in Italy.

It makes me angry and sad at the same time. Deceptions, secrets, and long silences take their toll over time. I became good at burying it—call it denial—and channeled my energy into music instead. Music became the one place where I could express the unspeakable, transform the pain, and find some measure of clarity in the unknown.

The adoption was coordinated by Catholic Charities and the Catholic Committee for Refugees of the NCWC in Erie, Pennsylvania, in early 1959. I arrived in the U.S. officially labeled an "orphan." My adoptive parents said they contacted their local Catholic church in Oil City to inquire about adoption. But because they were in their early forties, they were told they were too old to adopt in the U.S. So, the church looked to Italy.

Their desires were fulfilled when a letter from the Department of Justice, dated March 16, 1959, confirmed their application had been approved.

My entry into a new life was sanctioned by paperwork I never saw as a child. An official letter from the U.S. Department of Justice approved my adoption as an orphan. Mom and Dad believed they were adopting an orphan. They had no idea of the Catholic Church's complicity in the scheme.

And what of the Italian authorities in Torino? A government office issued me an Italian passport and visa to fly to the United States. Were they complicit as well? After all, passports confirm your identity. I was a minor. Did someone lie on my behalf, informing authorities that my parents were dead, and I was an *orphan*? Who was this person? Was Rosanna deceived as well?

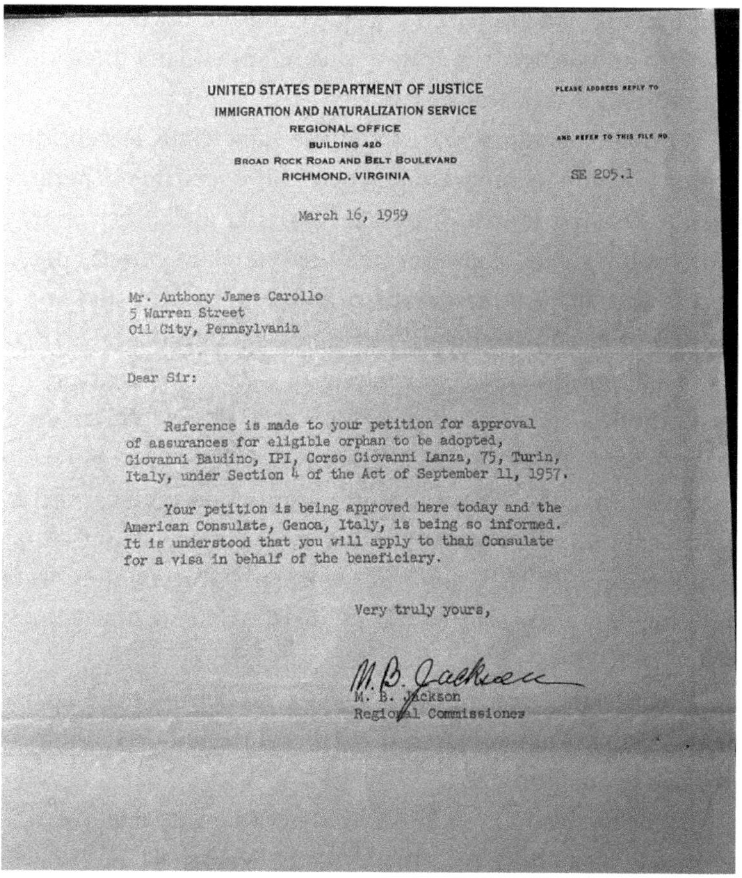
UNITED STATES DEPARTMENT OF JUSTICE
IMMIGRATION AND NATURALIZATION SERVICE
REGIONAL OFFICE
BUILDING 420
BROAD ROCK ROAD AND BELT BOULEVARD
RICHMOND, VIRGINIA

PLEASE ADDRESS REPLY TO
AND REFER TO THIS FILE NO.
SE 205.1

March 16, 1959

Mr. Anthony James Carollo
5 Warren Street
Oil City, Pennsylvania

Dear Sir:

Reference is made to your petition for approval of assurances for eligible orphan to be adopted, Giovanni Baudino, IPI, Corso Giovanni Lanza, 75, Turin, Italy, under Section 4 of the Act of September 11, 1957.

Your petition is being approved here today and the American Consulate, Genoa, Italy, is being so informed. It is understood that you will apply to that Consulate for a visa in behalf of the beneficiary.

Very truly yours,

M. B. Jackson
M. B. Jackson
Regional Commissioner

*Official letter from the U.S. Department of Justice approving my adoption as an orphan.*

In July 2006, Bill and I flew to Italy for the premiere of one of my works. We visited the former infant facility—La nuova sede dell'Istituto Provinciale per l'Infanzia at Corso Giovanni Lanza, 75. The gates were locked. A passerby translated for us: The institute was closed that day, but we could return tomorrow. We did.

The next morning, we met forensic social worker Enzo

Genco and his staff. He told us my mother had explicitly requested not to be contacted, though I saw no written documentation of that fact. He could not release identifying information. Enzo stated that Rosanna not only breastfed me but also worked at the facility.

He handed me a photo identical to the one in my original Italian passport. He also gave me the address of a local court and suggested I write for assistance.

Lorenzo disputes these records. He believes I was taken from our mother and given to a "rich" family. But if that were true, why would they place me in an infant institute? His account doesn't align with what I have been told. He insists our mother always wanted me—and that she carried a photo of me in her purse her entire life. He says that the photo was buried with her.

Perhaps she did carry such pain. Perhaps she never forgave herself. Perhaps she was tricked. Or perhaps she believed the story she had to believe in.

Back in Honolulu, I wrote the letter to the court, translated into Italian. A year later, I received a reply, but it was in Italian, and I couldn't understand it. A friend translated it for me. It stated that no adoption order had ever been recorded. No file. No record.

The court's decision read: "There are no reasons for proceeding ... No file at this Court concerning an adoption case involving the appellant."

Another disappointment in a long line of them.

To Lorenzo, this was proof I had been stolen. To me, it was further evidence of Italian bureaucratic disarray. No record does not mean no event. Perhaps the Church simply didn't want a paper trail.

What do I believe?

I believe my mother, unable to support both me and her aging mother, either chose to give me up or was manipulated into it. She nursed me. She loved me in her way. And eventually, she surrendered to circumstances she could not change. I believe she carried that pain to her grave.

Josephine later sent me a photo I had never seen—of me standing alone in the nunnery. I look lost. Sad. How she got the photo remains a mystery. Did Rosanna take it? Did she know where I was all along?

I returned to Italy again in October 2022, hoping for answers. But the adoption was never discussed—not by my brother, not by my sister. Not my mother's reasons. Not the separation. We communicated using Google Translate, but what we meant was often lost—and, with it, our chance to be clearly understood.

Lorenzo and Giusy showed me the house where Rosanna lived with her mother, pregnant with me. It was surreal. I felt mixed emotions. It was real.

And so, the mystery remains.

# CHAPTER 2

## Adopted Life in Pennsylvania: Ghosts of an Italian Boyhood

Oil City, Pennsylvania, was a place of hilly terrain, oil derricks, and quiet routines. My childhood unfolded in that small industrial town where my adoptive parents, Tony and Mary Carollo, lived modestly and spoke an Italian dialect I did not understand. I was a quiet child—timid, observant, and inward. English became my language, but my earliest inner voice knew only silence, sensation, and sound.

I can recall daydreaming often as I transitioned to a new language. How do you explain yourself when no one in kindergarten speaks Italian? Being misunderstood cultivates a quiet reserve, where sensation—especially sound—becomes heightened. I still have a keen sense of hearing to this day.

The rustle of branches swaying in the trees, birds chirping in rhythmic bursts, the steady tick of the cuckoo clock—these were not just background noise; they were sensations I noticed with intensity.

I loved the flutter of comic book pages, the soft crackle of a record spinning on our old 78-player, the low growl of the engine as we barreled down the highway in Dad's '57 Chevy. All of them left an imprint. These sounds weren't just ambient—they were formative. They tuned my ears. They shaped the musical sensibilities that would define me later in life.

In reflection, I realize my new home lacked essentials: musical instruments, books, and art. I treasure these now and often wonder how my life might have changed had they been present early on. Might I have been composing at age eight?

But I've learned that living in the present is where good mental health resides, so I try not to regret.

Still, something was already forming within me in those impressionable years—something that predated my arrival in America. Perhaps it was planted in the silent years in the nunnery above Torino. Perhaps solitude became a seed. Deprived of answers about my past, I grew up in an interior world that later gave birth to music.

On December 12, 1960, a judge handed down the decree of adoption. From that day forward, I would be known as John Anthony Carollo. My adoptive parents rarely spoke of my birth name. All I knew was that in Italy I had once been called Giovanni—an orphan. Being told I was "adopted from Italy" became both a badge of origin and a quiet scar I bore alone. The photo inside my Italian passport, taken before my journey on flight ICEM-12992, showed me wearing hand-me-down clothes. I looked sad, lonely, and solemn. Haunted. I didn't ask any questions. I turned inward instead.

Full of wonder about my new life and with so much to discover, I became curious about my new environment, my newfound family, and the playmates in the neighborhood. I took frequent walks to the local grocery store. There, I would choose from a wide variety of comic books where text merged with illustrations. I brought comics home and became immersed in worlds of action heroes and detective fiction—each a vivid escape into imagination.

The fusion of words and pictures brought stories to life in a way pure text alone could not—each page was an adventure; each hero was a reflection of my hopes, fears, or dreams. These comic books were more than entertainment. I now know that they nurtured my love for storytelling, sharpened my sense of

*The solemn boy in hand-me-downs, soon to be renamed.*

right and wrong, and gave me a place to process emotions too big for words alone. In those worlds of caped crusaders and shadowy villains, I found dilemmas that mirrored the moral complexities of life.

Also, in the quiet aisle of that grocery store, I found a small sense of ownership and independence—choosing my own stories, spending my own change, stepping into realms that both comforted and challenged me.

Learning a new language was more important to me than reminiscing about what might have been. I remember being a lonely child, however, and while there were moments of happiness, they were outweighed by stretches of sadness and quiet despair. Deep down, I longed for a sibling—someone to share secrets with, to play board games with on rainy days. But my adoptive parents never adopted again. I was left to figure out life on my own, learning to relate to others one awkward step at a time.

Frequent yearly trips to Rome, New York, where both sides of my family lived and where my mother was born, offered a welcome escape from dreary Oil City. I remember my Aunt Lena, my mother's sister, as a caring person who truly listened and, I firmly believe, understood me. I learned decades later that she had opposed the adoption. She told Mom and Dad they were too old and ill-equipped to raise a child. Aunt Lena lost the battle.

Being raised by parents old enough to be grandparents was not easy. My mother had dropped out of school in the eighth grade due to poor eyesight. My father, Tony, a high school graduate, was an alcoholic who gave me little time or attention. His life followed a strict routine: wake early, eat breakfast, go to work, return home, nap, dinner, beer, television—night after night, year after year. Then, off to bed. He and my mother had separate bedrooms. I often wondered if they had ever consummated their marriage. I doubt they did. One night, I heard him enter her room, only to be rejected. She was frigid and fearful of sex. I came to blame religion. She wanted to emulate the Virgin Mary in all things.

I don't believe my mother was ever truly happy. I suspect she married to avoid becoming an old maid. My father seemed to live in quiet resentment; his silences were weighted with discontent. He worked a monotonous job in the shipping department of the Chicago Pneumatic Tool Co., packing parts for boats and plane engines. It wore him down. He never earned much, but he had been born in the house we lived in, so he never paid rent. That gave him a rare sense of stability. When they didn't want me to understand, they slipped into Italian—leaving me outside the circle of meaning, a dialect I didn't know. It made me feel excluded.

I learned early on that being an outsider was my natural state, a kind of sanctuary I could retreat into when the world proved too harsh.

My adoptive parents gave me love, yes, and a roof over my head, but something vital was always missing. Tony never took me to a ballgame, never taught me to fish or bowl, never showed interest in the kinds of activities children long for. There were no family games, no chess or checkers to draw us together. Instead, there was distance. Emotional quiet. I grew to resent him.

They had no musical background. There was no piano in the parlor, though we did have a record player. Dad had a collection of 78s with Italian popular songs. No classical music. One of his pleasures was listening to the radio, pop tunes mostly, and I would join him. He listened silently, and I mirrored his behavior, sitting quietly beside him.

My mother paid more attention. She read to me and was always gentle. But she was devoutly Catholic, almost to the point of fanaticism. Each night, she had me kneel and pray before the small altar just outside my bedroom door. For a time, she attended daily Mass and worked part-time cleaning the rectory at St. Joseph's Parish. She'd come home shaking her head, whispering that the priests "drank too much."

As a cook, she wasn't particularly skilled. Most of her food was dry and overcooked, though I did enjoy her veal cutlets and pasta. Her tomato sauces were flavorful and remain vivid in my memory. But her true gift was baking. When visiting relatives in Rome, NY, she would bring large cans filled with cookies. She even sold cookies to neighbors. I helped mix ingredients and clean up afterward. My favorites were her fig-filled and orange cookies. Her cookies weren't just delicious—they were beautiful. In that respect, Mary was an artist.

My father's only passion was gardening. That was something we did together. Each spring, I helped him plant vegetables. All summer, we would harvest them. In the evenings, my parents would spend hours in the basement canning food for the long winters.

Another pastime was poker with his side of the family, a game of mathematical probabilities. I often won, even with nickel antes. I remember the joy I felt seeing the large pile of coins. Mother never did well. Dad won occasionally. His smile, in those rare moments, was a welcome relief from his otherwise grim demeanor.

Living in a predominantly Polish, working-class neighborhood, I quickly lost the language I was born with. I now regret that loss deeply. When I met my half-brother and sister in 2022, it would have meant so much to speak with them in their native tongue.

Amid these early impressions and routines, a shadow crept in. I can't pinpoint exactly when I lost my confidence, but it happened early—somewhere in the ache of childhood.

I went to St. Joseph's Grade School, where the nuns taught with stern discipline. Some were kind, others were less so. I remember a boy named Tony. We both loved to draw and would pass sketches back and forth in class. One day, we were caught. The nuns confiscated and destroyed our drawings. We were punished instead of encouraged. I never returned to drawing after that. It was one of the first times I felt the sting of how artistic wonder can be killed in childhood.

Grade school was difficult. I was shy and uncertain. I often felt different from the other children but couldn't explain why. Was it my early attraction to boys? There was always a sense of being slightly out of place—too sensitive, too inward. Was listening to that inner voice of shame healthy? I began to escape into dreams, into books, into drawing—and, later, into music. My inner life became more real than the outer world.

As I matured into adulthood, I discovered that listening to the voice of shame can be an act of courage. It is a confrontation with shadow, a step toward integration, and a path to truth. I needed to become aware of it—to recognize where it was coming from, what it was saying, and how it was shaping my life.

When we ignore or silence shame completely, it continues to operate beneath the surface, unchecked. But listening to it with awareness allows us to pause, reflect, and ultimately reframe the story. This understanding helped me grow stronger, more compassionate, and to be able to give and receive love, including with a life partner.

I did have childhood friends. The Moran family lived across the street. Ann Moran, who cut my mother's hair, had a sharp sense of humor and told wonderful stories during her visits. Her daughter, Barbara, became a friend and confidant. Her son, Jimmy, and I spent many weekends at the YMCA, where we learned to swim, play billiards, and attend summer camps.

The three of us—Barbara, Jimmy, and I—would go ice skating every Friday night at the large rink in Hasson Heights. We'd skate for hours under the lights, laughing and gliding across the ice. One of my favorite treats at the rink was the vinegar-soaked French fries—salty, tangy, and unforgettable.

I also remember playing touch football with neighborhood boys. One afternoon, my good friend Don was badly injured. I helped him home, but he collapsed in the street. I ran to alert his parents. He had ruptured his spleen and was bleeding internally. My quick action saved his life. I gave up football not long after. I had been shoved into a jagged concrete wall, requiring hernia surgery and a long recovery.

In fourth or fifth grade, I began piano lessons with a musical nun who had selected a handful of students she believed had potential. That was the quiet beginning—though I wouldn't grasp its true significance until years later, when music finally took hold of me.

# PART II

## Awakenings

# CHAPTER 3

## Awakening the Inner Musician

A seemingly insignificant moment in fourth or fifth grade quietly marked the beginning of a lifelong path—piano lessons with a nun who sensed something in me I didn't yet understand. I followed her into the convent music room, where a well-worn baby grand piano waited for my hesitant first attempts at playing.

Weekly lessons meant walking several miles to the convent to practice and learn. I remember the John Thompson lesson books—the red-covered volumes through which countless young musicians absorbed theory, technique, and gradually more complex repertoire. I enjoyed learning new pieces, but no one helped shape the broader path.

I still recall the smell of that small room—polished wood and old sheet music. The feel of the keys beneath my fingers was unfamiliar at first, but soon curiosity took over. I wasn't composing yet; I was discovering. Something stirred inside me that had no name, no form. But it was real. Music wasn't entering me; it was awakening within me.

Long before those lessons, I had been building an inner world. My imagination, pencil drawings, and vivid dreams were not distractions—they were training grounds. In a home without a piano, without musicians to emulate, and with little stimulation beyond *Reader's Digest* magazines for the blind (both my parents had poor eyesight—Tony was legally blind, though he still drove to work), imagination became my sanctuary.

I lived there. It was a kind of dreaming that didn't end upon waking. It carried me through the days, even as I knelt for the rosary before bedtime.

I began to hear melodies in my head that had no source. I didn't yet know how to write them down, but they haunted me gently, like whispers from a parallel world.

That was when I bought an acoustic guitar. My friends were deep into English and American folk-rock—bands like Fairport Convention and solo artists like Richard Thompson. I was swept up in it, too.

I'd walk over to Moose's house—Terry Rodgers, a peculiar and kind soul I met in front of a soda pop store in Oil City. He stood there nightly, gazing into the dark. Tall and lean, Moose had dropped out of school early. A birth defect left him with a weak heart, requiring open-heart surgery as a child. A tiny mustache gave him a touch of Groucho Marx.

Every afternoon after school, we'd listen to records and strum guitars. Moose became a true friend. We understood each other. We knew music could transform us; lift us to a place where early sorrows no longer seemed to matter. It was heaven on earth.

Moose died shortly after I moved to California at age twenty-one. I will never forget the day Terry Anthony, another friend addicted to music, called to report the sad news. I silently wept, acknowledging that what I had with Moose could not be recreated.

My desire to understand music grew slowly through adolescence. I spent what I earned from part-time jobs on records—gold to me. I studied album covers, liner notes, and band members' names. These weren't just records; they were maps to other realms, clues to uncovering creative truth.

That's when my passion for collecting began. I listened to acoustic guitar records published by Kicking Mule and Takoma Records. John Fahey, a pioneering fingerstyle guitarist and founder of the American Primitive Guitar style, was—and remains—a favorite guitar maestro. American and English folk music fascinated me, especially the rich English tradition of ballads and songs stretching back hundreds of years.

Classical music followed. Through those early piano lessons at St. Joseph's, I discovered the extraordinary worlds of Bach and Beethoven. I wanted to be J.S. Bach. One of my early piano preludes is entitled "*B Bach*."

Looking back, I now believe solitude was my greatest teacher. The absence of company became the condition for musical thought. The isolation I felt as an only child, raised by aging parents who lived more in habit than expression, paradoxically created space for those first creative murmurings. I honor that now, at age seventy.

Solitude and spontaneity: both are prerequisites for creativity. I didn't know this then, but it became clear in the years when composing turned from routine to necessity.

Church music also seeped into me—not just the melodies, but the emotions behind them. I joined the church choir and loved singing. The solemnity, the reverence, the way the human voice rose to meet something beyond itself—these moments stirred me.

Hearing hymns and sacred music during weekly Mass shaped my emotional and creative compass. I began to understand that music wasn't merely entertainment. It was a language of feeling. It spoke truths no conversation could. It conveyed emotion, stories, and insights into the human condition. It expanded my emotional vocabulary and, with it, the range of what I could express.

*The quiet house.*
*The devout mother.*
*The withdrawn father.*
*The restless kneeling at church.*
*The backyard vegetable garden.*
*The missing siblings.*
*The Polish neighborhood.*
*The lost Italian tongue.*
*The sketchbook destroyed by the nuns.*
*The musical companions curious about the arts.*

All of it became part of the musical vocabulary I would one day draw inspiration from. Not yet in musical notes, but in emotional gestures. In silences. In longings.

By the time I began piano lessons, music already had a home in me. The nun may have taught me scales and sight-reading, but she could not teach me what was already growing there. That was mine. That was memory. That was survival.

In hindsight, I see now: I was not learning music—I was remembering it.

Music was my original language. The first tongue I spoke in silence, before words came. It lived in me. And once named, it would never leave.

# CHAPTER 4
## The Adolescent Composer

Adolescence brought new challenges. I was aware that my attraction to men, present since age six, grew stronger each year. After puberty, I realized this attraction wasn't considered "normal" by other boys in grade school or high school. Like many gay men of my generation, I hid. I stayed in the closet, keeping my truth a secret to avoid being picked on, verbally abused, spat upon, or shunned. The internal dialogue was relentless, whispering inside me: *Everyone I see is straight. I must emulate them. I cannot be authentic. What will Mom and Dad say? I cannot be me.*

That fear of rejection stifled authenticity, creativity, and emotional growth. So, I buried myself in academics, excelling in math and science. Solving algebraic equations on the blackboard became my way of proving worth—to myself and to others. I modeled myself after the brightest students, took homework seriously, and pursued scholastic excellence with quiet determination.

Ending piano lessons in eighth grade left a quiet void. Music had been a refuge—a language of feeling I hadn't yet learned to name. I turned instead to science fiction novels, dated a few girls to appear "normal," and attended the occasional party. Still, I felt restless and uneasy. I went to the prom with a shy girl who, fittingly, later became a nun. Even then, I knew I was different. I began seeking the company of other gay men, though few were visible in our small town.

In 1972, just after graduating from Oil City Area High School, I walked into Wallace Book Store. A large paperback caught my eye: *Amphigorey*, the first collected works of Edward Gorey. I took it home and read it cover to cover. I was hooked. My love affair with all things Gorey continues to this day.

Convincing my parents to let me have a dog turned out to be a mistake. Dad kept Frodo in the cellar, as Mom believed animals were "dirty." But Frodo—named after the *Lord of the Rings* character—became a quiet source of comfort during this uncertain time.

Around then, I began writing poetry. It became a safe haven, a space where I could express emotions I couldn't share with friends or family. I could never discuss my desires with my devoutly religious parents. I couldn't explain my feelings to musical friends who assumed I was straight. Writing was the only place I could be honest.

Leaving home to attend Penn State Behrend wasn't driven by ambition—it was escape. I needed to get away from Oil City, from parents who didn't know how to nurture confidence. But Behrend proved isolating. Though I dated a girl I thought I might love, the relationship went nowhere. I was fooling myself again. Then Dad called to tell me he had run over Frodo, who had to be put down. The sadness deepened. My focus drifted.

Returning home, I convinced my parents to buy an upright piano and resumed lessons. This reignited something in me. There is something uniquely satisfying about the feel of keys beneath one's fingers, the discipline of reading and memorizing music, and the emotional release of performance. Though my new teacher struggled with alcohol, she saw my talent and encouraged me to prepare for a competition in Pittsburgh.

I won National Honors. The story appeared in *The Derrick*, our local paper. I still have the pin I was awarded—a small token of a major triumph.

At my first public recital, I froze halfway through a difficult piece, but only for a moment. I recovered, finished strong, and the applause gave me hope. What no one knew was what had just happened before the concert. On my way there, I had followed a handsome man I suspected was gay. He led me to an isolated park; aware I was trailing him, I got out and said hello, seeing his beautiful face. Startled by the time, I hurried off to my performance. That fleeting moment taught me something I hadn't fully realized: it was possible to be gay—and happy and at peace.

I knew I had to leave Oil City. Its small-town outlook and narrow values were suffocating. Depression set in, followed by suicidal thoughts. My musical friends were dating. I was isolated, frightened, and confused. Alcohol and marijuana became my escape from deep feelings of insecurity, self-loathing, uncertainty, low self-esteem, and loneliness.

One night, I broke down in front of my mother, begging her to let me go. Dad had always insisted I remain home until I turned twenty-one. Mom understood. She persuaded him to let me leave.

In 1976, at age twenty-one, I moved to San Diego. It marked a pivotal transition—a moment when the past loosened its grip, and the future stepped forward. I carried the weight of my childhood in Oil City, the early stirrings of music, and a longing that had never abated. San Diego, with its warm Pacific air, open horizons, and golden light, felt like an exhale after years of holding my breath.

The invitation came from Robbie, an acquaintance I met

while working at Polk State Hospital after my short stay at Behrend. He called San Diego "paradise" and urged me to come live with him and taste freedom. Several co-workers at the hospital, aware of my plan, said I would never make it. Unknown to them was my perseverance. Completing what I start—and taking on challenges—has always been essential to my identity.

So, I moved. But within days, I was robbed of $1,200—my savings. I had hidden the money in my room and, foolishly, showed it to Robbie. When it vanished, I moved out and into the home of a truck driver I had just met, who kindly offered me shelter.

Then everything changed. Three weeks later, I met Bill.

We met at Black's Beach, a nude beach with unspoken boundaries: straights on one side, gays on the other. It was liberating to be myself without judgment. I had been there before, but that day, I paused at the cliff's edge to have a cigarette. A tall, handsome man approached and asked for one. Our eyes met. Something sparked and never dimmed. That man was Bill.

He invited me to dinner. Following him in my old Corvette, I felt something I hadn't felt in years: joy.

Ours became a partnership grounded in affection, mutual respect, and quiet understanding. Bill, a psychiatrist trained in Heidelberg, Germany, worked at San Diego County Mental Health. He was brilliant, well-read, worldly—everything my father was not. His love of art, architecture, and history complemented my passion for music and writing. He gave me stability and encouragement. The thirty-year age difference never mattered. We saw each other clearly.

One of our first projects was restoring the Ira Floyd House in National City. The mansion on Highland Avenue had fallen into disrepair. Breathing life into it became a metaphor for my own transformation. We restored the home and the carriage house in the backyard. As we stripped away decay and revealed beauty beneath, I, too, began to feel uncovered.

Music returned—not as fantasy, but as discipline. I resumed piano lessons. Bill even bought a seven-foot grand piano, sight unseen. It was nearly impossible to keep in tune, but it became my sanctuary.

San Diego City College soon followed. I enrolled with dreams of studying music, but found myself equally drawn to psychology. How sound affects memory, identity, and emotion—how trauma and creativity intertwine—these questions fascinated me. I pursued both disciplines, driven by curiosity.

There, I met Dr. Jim Paul, a theory professor who encouraged my musical abilities. He introduced me to a new piano teacher. Soon, I was studying a piece by Domenico Scarlatti. I told my instructor, Robert Haffenden, that I could compose something similar. He was skeptical. A week later, I returned with a completed manuscript—my first solo piano piece. Scarlatti was the spark that lit the fire. I became a composer. A creator. I discovered I could mold sound into forms that expressed inner truth.

After receiving an associate's degree, I enrolled at San Diego State University (SDSU). Academia gave me what I'd never known: a structured space for exploration. I devoured readings, asked questions, and trusted my instincts. Beneath it all, the music waited—simmering.

Psychology loomed large, too. I wanted to understand myself and others more deeply. One professor, Dr. Shay, introduced me to George Kelly's work. His *Psychology of Personal Constructs* (1955) changed my life. Kelly proposed that what people say belongs to them—it is part of their personal construct system. Their words are often more about themselves than others.

This was a revelation: *You are your personal constructs.*

With a greater sense of self-awareness, I pursued a master's degree in clinical psychology. While completing my graduate thesis, I composed my first piece of music.

1986 marked the beginning of a long love affair with musical composition.

During that time, a female classmate asked me to father her child. She promised to raise the baby on her own, with no strings attached. I turned her down, not fully grasping the magnitude of what she was asking but knowing I could not betray Bill's love and trust. I could not create life without intention. She understood.

San Diego in the 1980s was a city of contrasts—bohemian and military, sprawling yet intimate. I remember the scent of eucalyptus, the golden light at dusk, and the hum of freeways behind ocean breezes. It became the backdrop for my renaissance.

No longer just the adopted boy from Italy. No longer just the lonely child from Oil City. I was a student, a partner, a seeker. My identity, long fragmented, began to cohere. This was the foundation.

The roots I planted in San Diego would support everything that came next—the composer, the poet, the solitary dreamer.

The Ira Floyd Mansion still stands, catching the Pacific light like I did then:

*Open. Restored. Radiant.*

# CHAPTER 5

## Adult Responsibilities and Private Creation

The piano from San Francisco was an old beauty—its polished wood glowing in the filtered light that spilled through our Victorian windows. It took its place in the large living room of the hundred-year-old mansion Bill and I were restoring, a room that seemed to hold whispers of the past in every corner. Sitting down with a pad and pencil, the act of turning fleeting inspiration into notes on a staff felt as natural as breathing. The music flowed out of me, sometimes one piece a day, sometimes several, as if the piano had been waiting all along for my hands to awaken its voice. The outside world faded during those mornings—schoolwork and home repairs could wait. The quiet sanctuary of our home pulsed with possibility.

Bill was my anchor through it all. He didn't need to understand every musical phrase or nuance to know what it meant to me. His faith in my process and the value of my work wrapped around me like a warm blanket. We fell into a rhythm—a pattern of quiet mornings at the piano, afternoons spent editing scores, and evenings walking beneath San Diego's golden light. The city's soft breeze and the mellow hum of distant traffic became the backdrop for the composer I was quietly becoming, and the man I was becoming in partnership with Bill.

Between 1986 and 1997, I composed solo piano pieces without formal instruction, guided only by instinct and my own ear. These earliest works were small in scale but vast in personal significance—musical confessions I had long held inside. At the piano, I communed with memory, intuition, and something deeper—something I can only describe as the unknown reaching through my fingers.

Ideas came unannounced—a motif, a cluster of chords, a rhythm that demanded attention. I learned to honor these gifts, to follow where they led me, even when the path was unclear. I didn't call myself a composer yet—just a person thrilled to complete a piece that quieted an inner restlessness. It was a calling I barely understood, a compulsion to fulfill something essential inside me.

Years later, I would gather these "little gems" and group them as *Early Piano Works* on my website, www.johncarollocomposer.com. Revising them took years—a slow sharpening of each phrase, often in the shadow of larger ensemble pieces.

Bob, the composition teacher who would later become a mentor, once told me these early pieces belonged in the trash—good only as garbage liners—recalling how some great composers discarded their first efforts out of sheer dissatisfaction. He even mentioned Gustav Mahler, whose wife Alma later claimed to have disposed of his early manuscripts, which Mahler himself reportedly did not value.

At the time, I wondered if Bob was right. Maybe my early sketches deserved the same fate. But I couldn't bring myself to part with them. To me, those first musical scribbles were the raw, honest beginnings of a journey. Keeping them—flaws and all—let me trace how a musical language evolves, how innocence shifts toward insight, how the simplest phrase can spark a path to something astonishing.

As I began editing the *Early Piano Works*, some pieces gained new titles to match their refined shapes; others were pared down until their true essence emerged. Listening back through the MIDI interface, I heard the difference: more excitement, more substance, more strength.

One evening, Bill came home from work with his eyes burning with rage. He was dismissed from his role as a psychiatrist at the county hospital after openly challenging administrators during a State-monitored meeting. His identity, long rooted in his work with patients struggling with severe mental illness, suddenly felt insecure and uncertain.

He spent the night on urgent calls to colleagues, searching for a way forward. Rudy, a friend in the mental health field, offered him a position as an outpatient psychiatrist in El Centro, a small desert town several hours away. Bill accepted, though the new job meant we'd be separated during the week, seeing each other only on weekends. I stayed in National City, holding down the home front.

At the same time, I was caring for my aging parents. Dad needed cataract surgery, and Mom, caught in the relentless grip of Alzheimer's, required daily support. I had noticed the slow erosion of her memory even before leaving Oil City. Years earlier, during my first job bagging groceries in Oil City, I called her from the break room. Her voice was distant and confused. When she didn't recognize me, I raised my voice, thinking she couldn't hear. But it wasn't her hearing—it was her memory slipping away like sand through fingers.

Caring for Mom became a quiet ritual. Each morning, I bathed her, stripped and washed soiled linens, dressed her carefully, and made breakfast. Once she was settled, the day moved forward against a backdrop of frequent trips to the bathroom and moments of confusion. Dad came home from surgery, a little stronger but still fragile. Returning them to their home in Rome, New York, brought some relief, though a deep sadness lingered. Knowing Dad would care for Mom alone until her death in 1990 weighed heavily on me. I still miss Mary.

Selling the Floyd House was a wrenching decision. We had poured five years into restoring it—a labor of love and sweat. The foundation was reinforced, the roofs repaired, and the floors were polished until they gleamed like mirrors. Water damage in the carriage house was repaired—electrical systems modernized, plumbing redone. Historical details—the rooftop widow's walk, original windows, ornate fireplace mantels, and hearth tiles—were preserved or carefully reconstructed. We patched plaster walls, strengthened ceilings, and renovated kitchens and bathrooms, always balancing respect for history with the demands of modern living. Even the landscaping was planned with care, designed to echo the home's architectural soul.

I worked alongside Bill every step of the way, exchanging my labor for his financial support of my education. I was unemployed, but the work grounded me.

Chuck, Bill's adopted son, visited from time to time. His battles with alcoholism had caused Bill deep pain before I entered the picture. Chuck had a charm that could disarm but was often opportunistic, taking advantage of goodwill without remorse.

Bill's past was complicated. He had divorced Elfy, a woman he met while studying medicine in Heidelberg. They had lived in Napa, where Bill practiced psychiatry. Together, they had two children—a boy and a girl—but as Bill's latent homosexuality became impossible to hide, Elfy asked for a divorce. She eventually remarried a psychologist Bill introduced her to.

Susan, Bill's daughter, lived with us while attending San Diego State University—at the same time I was enrolled there. Elfy had no idea. According to Susan, her mother painted Bill as a monster. Her brother Thomas remained quiet and distant. Elfy's new husband legally adopted both children, a choice that tore at Bill's heart and identity.

Bill suffered years of quiet anguish over the loss of his children. The legal name change struck a deep psychological blow to his identity as a father—a wound that never fully healed. I bottled up the atmosphere of his suffering and later poured it into *Anguish in Every Household for Orchestra* (2008–2010), included in my *Starry Night* (2011) release.

Program Notes (included in the score): *This work was transcribed from the second movement of my Piano Suite No. 4 for 3 Pianos (2005). It attempts to capture the suffering that seems constant in human relationships. When I conceived this music, several close friends were enduring turmoil, severe mental or physical pain. The music is to be played with as much anguish, pain, and sorrow as possible. Pedal markings for piano and celesta serve as guides only. My musical aesthetics welcome performer interpretation. Dynamic ranges are suggestions intended to work well as written. —JAC*

*Note: Place chimes and tam-tam as far apart as possible.*

I wanted to give voice to what often goes unsaid in families fractured by time, trauma, or misunderstanding. In Bill's case, it was the loss of his children, the misrepresentation of his character, and the silence imposed on that relationship.

After we sold the Floyd House, we moved to El Centro. The desert air was dry and relentless, the sun unyielding. I found work as a conservator and case manager, a job that demanded both compassion and strict judgment. I assessed the needs of gravely disabled individuals, selected placements ranging from community homes to locked facilities when necessary, and provided informed consent for mental health treatments—even over the objections of those I served. It was challenging and humbling work. I was honored with special recognition for saving the county money by successfully discharging patients from state hospitals and finding more appropriate levels of care.

Through all the heat and dust, one truth remained: I needed to compose. The piano from San Francisco traveled with us, its worn keys whispering of home and continuity.

Then came the early-morning earthquake—a sudden shaking that rattled our nerves and unsettled our world. It was a jolt—a reminder that even solid ground can fracture without warning.

That day, we made a decision that would alter the course of our lives. We would leave California behind. We would move to Hawai‘i.

On that island paradise, surrounded by ocean and sky, we would spend many years building a life together—falling more deeply in love with each passing year, and watching my career as a composer blossom under the tropical sun.

# CHAPTER 6

## Coming into Myself

## THE MUSICAL COMPOSITION

*To craft a composition to perfection*
*requires both skill and creative invention.*

*Knowing one's aesthetic values*
*determines the unique outcome.*

*Persistence in shaping your artful design*
*into a work of lasting value pays dividends:*

*The listener is taken into a sonic ride*
*through the artist's unconscious mind.*

It was 1987. We were on our way to O'ahu, our home for the next twenty-seven years—a new chapter in life, and the beginning of a creative rebirth that would define my identity as a composer. High above the Pacific, the jumbo jet hummed steadily, wings slicing through endless blue. Fortune favored us that day—an overbooked flight meant we were upgraded to first class. I remember the thrill of sinking into plush leather seats, the soft clink of glasses in the cabin, and the pilot's unexpected visit. When he shook our hands, listened to our story, and announced over the speakers that we were moving to O'ahu, the entire plane erupted in applause. It felt like the universe was welcoming us.

We rented a small apartment on Pualei Circle, nestled at the base of Diamond Head. Cozy and well-situated, it was just a short stroll from Queen's Beach, where we swam each morning in the warm Pacific waters. Our one-bedroom space opened easily to Kapiʻolani Park and Waikiki Beach, where the air was forever scented with salt and tropical blooms. Shopping in Waikiki was a joy—just ten minutes on foot—where local artists showcased paintings and crafts inspired by golden sunlight and the island's endless warmth.

We donated the grand piano from San Diego to the Hawaiʻi State Hospital (HSH). Watching it go felt like letting go of a chapter in my musical journey—a moment both melancholic and necessary. It marked a transition, not a loss, as I made space for something new to arrive. Watching it unloaded from the moving van and lifted onto a truck was bittersweet. But soon after, I fulfilled a dream—I bought a Steinway baby grand. Its warm, rich sound and responsive keys felt like the perfect partner.

With the Steinway in place, I resumed composing miniature piano pieces, my enthusiasm fueled by the vibrant, tropical backdrop. Doubts about the worth of my work still flickered, but I had enough confidence to keep going. The music was a calling I couldn't ignore, a voice rising from somewhere deep within.

Bill quickly secured a contract psychiatrist position with the State of Hawaiʻi. He traveled to Maui and Molokaʻi, serving patients in remote communities—including the former leprosy colony. I took a position as a sex abuse counselor in Waiʻanae, a close-knit town rich with Native Hawaiian culture and natural beauty.

After two years, an unsettling incident—a client's inappropriate advance—prompted me to step away. I transitioned to a case manager role at a Department of Health satellite clinic in Kailua. From there, my public service career blossomed: social worker at HSH, head of statewide case management services, hospital liaison, provider relations specialist, and, finally, authorization officer for the Adult Mental Health Division (AMHD).

A friend of Bill's from work invited us to join the Hawaiian Lodge. I worked my way up through the chairs and became Master of the Lodge in 1996. Bill followed in 1997, with me as Secretary. Throughout those years, and later in the Shriners, no one ever asked about our relationship. No one seemed curious. It was like living a double life: one as a loving gay couple, the other cloaked in silence within a mystical world where secrets were sacred—ours included.

Looking back, I wonder what it meant to be present but unseen. The Lodge was steeped in ritual and symbols layered with hidden meanings. Yet the meaning of our love remained unspoken, quietly folded into the fabric of accepted silence. We were never rejected, but neither were we fully known. That silence was both a shield and a sorrow. In those solemn halls, we belonged—but only in part. It taught me that secrecy can feel like safety, but over time, it exacts a price: the cost of not being fully seen.

Around that time, I composed *Themes for Edward Gorey* (1996), a multi-movement solo piano work, a tentative translation of my inner world into sound. The music itself felt like a character, quirky and elusive, gently guiding me toward a voice I hadn't yet named.

The wife of one Lodge member asked to see the score. She liked it, recorded it to cassette, and encouraged me to study composition formally. She suggested I contact Robert Wehrman, fresh from earning his PhD in Music Composition at the University of Hawai'i at Manoa.

That phone call changed my life.

Robert asked to review my early piano pieces and encouraged me to compose something new for our next meeting. The beginnings of Opus 1: *Piano Suite No. 1 for Solo Piano (The Crumb Suite)* (1997) emerged from that challenge.

I recall struggling with this work. For years, my musical language had been tonal—it had to be, to understand harmony's rules, scales, and the central tonic note that holds everything in place. Why did cadences bring such satisfying resolution? I felt like I was unlocking the secret machinery behind the great masters' music.

But Bob challenged me. Competing with the masters was pointless, he said. "Get out of it," he urged. I wasn't fully convinced, but I was open to new ways of expression.

The suite's finale was a turning point—a complicated, expressive piece, straddling tonal boundaries without abandoning them. After hearing it, Bob said with certainty, "You've found your voice."

A daily rhythm settled in: early rising, breakfast and coffee, shower, full workday, dinner, then composing from 7 p.m., sometimes until 10 or later. This pattern held for years—until 2006, when a near-fatal car accident changed everything.

That same year, I retired from public service and founded Musica Baudino, dedicating myself wholly to composition.

Leaving my career wasn't dramatic. It arrived quietly, like many truths do—mirroring the quiet persistence of the music that had always lived within me, waiting for its full expression. I realized the moments I felt most alive were when I wrote music. I could no longer deny it. I wasn't just someone who composed. I was a composer.

Early on, Bob told me, "You're an artist." I looked at him, puzzled. Later, he confided that he and the Honolulu Symphony's second principal violinist, Darel Stark, agreed: I was no ordinary composer. There was something more. Something special.

That reshaped how I saw myself.

Yes, I had a master's degree in clinical psychology and years in mental health. That work gave me stability, a place in the world. But composition offered something deeper—a fusion of intellect, emotion, memory, and mystery. It helped me understand both the world around me and the one within. There were no commissions. No fame. No big checks in the mailbox. But there was something richer: Truth. Alignment. Purpose.

Some days, composing felt less like inspiration and more like necessity—a compulsion demanding release. I remember long nights crafting *Piano Suite No. 4 for 3 Pianos* (2005), a sprawling, technically challenging work that freed me emotionally. It wasn't a career, but a calling; every note answered a question I couldn't yet name. I composed because the music demanded it. If someone performed it, that was a gift—but the true reward was creation itself.

Still, I lived a double life. By day, a mental health counselor whose work attuned me to subtle shifts in language and silence—an attunement that would come to shape my musical sensitivity and deepen my appreciation for the unspoken. Listening deeply to others' pain, confusion, and resilience. That listening shaped my music. I came to see silence not as absence, but presence. In therapy and composition, the unspoken often carries the greatest weight.

I rarely submitted to calls for scores. I didn't want constraints—length, instrumentation, deadlines. That path wasn't mine. I didn't need music to survive. Bill never asked for rent. With his support, I could hire musicians to perform and record my work. I found a way to hear my music before I died.

Even in silence, I composed. Because I couldn't stop.

Solitude became a constant companion. In it, I found clarity. I embraced the belief that music is born in silence, in dreams, in deep inner listening. I came to see myself as a vessel. The music didn't come from me—it came through me. A mystical process. Not fully mine to own.

This was never a career. It was a calling. And once I answered it, there was no going back. I couldn't yet see the arc ahead—the recordings, the body of work, the recognition. But something had taken root. The music—patient, insistent, luminous—had begun to grow.

With each composition, I felt myself born anew—reborn through sound. The suite *Romantica Passione* (2004) for guitar and violin became a soundtrack to this renewal, its passionate dialogues reflecting the complexity of new relationships and inner growth. This phase of life was marked by a willingness to embrace beauty and dissonance, recognizing that creation often arises from tension.

# PART III

## Busy Being Born

# CHAPTER 7

## Musica Baudino and the Early Composition Years

It took months to complete *The Crumb Suite*, my Opus 1, but it began as a spark of curiosity—an impulse to honor the astonishing artistry of the Crumb family living in France. I'd long admired Robert Crumb's underground *Zap Comix*, whose subversive humor and raw honesty had shaped my early sense of creative rebellion. But I wanted to know more—what about the rest of the Crumb orbit?

I wrote to Aline, Robert's wife, not expecting a reply. To my surprise, she responded warmly and agreed to sell me one of her paintings. When the package arrived, I held the piece carefully in my hands—its colors vibrant, its energy immediate. That small connection reached deep inside me. It felt like a creative signal.

I then discovered Robert's brother, Maxon, whose publisher, Malcolm Whyte, helped me acquire several of his drawings. Maxon's art was the true revelation—raw, dynamic, profound, and delightfully strange. I saw in his work a kindred spirit.

I also acquired two original pieces by Robert's son Jesse, whose untimely death in a car accident years later hit me with unexpected sadness. And then came a collection of odd, joyful blue-ink drawings from their daughter Sophie—just ten or eleven at the time.

Surrounded by these visual treasures, inspiration struck me. I completed *The Crumb Suite* with a sense of arrival.

Then came *Frenetic Unfoldings for Solo Violin* (1998), a piece that seemed to erupt from within me. Bob was stunned—and so was I. It was my first masterpiece. He introduced me to Darel Stark, associate principal violinist with the Honolulu Symphony, who embraced the score wholeheartedly. We met several times to refine its technical demands.

*Frenetic Unfoldings* was atonal, shaped by Bob's introduction to Schoenberg's twelve-tone system. It was a demanding piece—intense, dissonant, and thrilling. We recorded it in a large church, its natural acoustics a perfect fit for the music's raw emotion. That piece remains a cornerstone of my catalogue.

Though I never fully embraced dodecaphony, its principles intrigued me—every pitch treated equally, no hierarchy. Atonal democracy. It felt like a kind of liberation. Bob often reminded me: I could never compete with Beethoven, Mozart, or Bach. "Get out of that tradition," he urged. "Forge your own path." But how?

Should I invent a new form altogether—something radical, complex, perhaps unlistenable? The mid-twentieth century had its share of music rooted in theory over feeling. Serialism reigned. Music became cerebral, often cold, and difficult to absorb.

Or should I write with simplicity—music that welcomed the listener?

The answer emerged slowly: I would speak from the heart. Spontaneous. Concise. Expressive. Authentic. This ethos eventually shaped my *Symphony No. 5* (2022–23), whose movement titles outlined a philosophy I had lived without realizing it:

- Triumph Over Obstacles
- Cherish Ideals
- Endure Loneliness
- Realize Aspirations

That was my roadmap all along.

Bob encouraged me to experiment with Messiaen's limited modes of transposition. They refer to a set of symmetrical scales that can only be transposed a limited number of times before repeating the same set of notes. These octatonic scales—containing eight notes per octave—are constructed through alternating whole and half steps (or vice versa). Often called "Messiaen Mode 2," these scales can only be transposed three times before the pitch collection repeats, due to their internal symmetry. Messiaen valued these modes for their unique harmonic and melodic possibilities, as their restricted transposability creates a sense of tonal ambiguity and color that resists traditional functional harmony.

Thus, my first quartet, *A Worded Grey Enigma* (2000), uses the octatonic scales for several of its movements, and I used them for other musical works during this time.

In 1998, under Bob's guidance, I composed *Woodwind Quintet No. 1 in Three Movements*—my first chamber work, later revised in 2012. It was around that time Bob insisted that every composition deserved a title. I was reluctant. Instrumental works by the old masters often bore only technical labels. But Bob was right: A good title was a doorway into meaning.

So, I began naming my pieces:

- *May I Have an Alchemist?*
- *My Dreams Lie Just Above the Horizon*
- *The Transfiguration of Giovanni Baudino*

By 1999, I began keeping a musical diary. I recorded rehearsal notes, score revisions, performance details—fragments of thought and feeling. I still write in it daily. That habit became a thread that wove through my creative life.

At the same time, I relied on my steady job at the AMHD. The hard truth loomed: Most professional performers rarely seek out new music. Musicians need to be paid. If I wanted my music to be heard, I had to become a composer, promoter, and patron all in one.

I often wondered: *How does one make a life in music? Is an audience necessary? Would they even want what I had to offer?* These questions unsettled me. It all felt fragile.

Bill, ever pragmatic, had warned me early on: "Music doesn't provide a comfortable life."

He was right—at least financially. But I pressed on. I knew this was my path, no matter how uncertain.

Then came the turning point.

Bill had just returned from visiting a dear friend in Thailand. I was helping a researcher at AMHD on a special project. One afternoon, I stepped outside for coffee. A dazed college student took a sharp turn around a large truck and crashed directly into my car.

The impact was ferocious. Smoke filled the vehicle. My fingers bled from shattered glass. I stumbled out, coughing, trying to call Bill—then collapsed on the sidewalk.

I awoke in the ER. Shards of glass were being removed from my knuckles—the pain was searing. I screamed involuntarily. When Bill arrived, his steady presence soothed me.

That trauma brought clarity.

What mattered more—my exhausting government job, or devoting myself to music? The answer was clear. That very evening, I told Bill I was resigning from civil service. He hugged me and simply said, "Go for it."

And so I did. My epiphany arrived unannounced, but its impact was profound—revealing a truth that shifted my course, not with fanfare, but with quiet, irreversible clarity.

# CHAPTER 8

## Out of Silence: The Birth of Ampersand

After moving out of the Diamond Head area, we bought a fixer-upper in Kailua, Hawai'i. I wanted to be close to my workplace, the Kailua Counseling Center, where I served as a case manager. While the psychiatrist and nurses stayed behind their office doors, working within the traditional model of care, I stepped out into the patients' worlds. I visited their homes, saw the worn furniture, the cluttered kitchens, the peeling paint on walls, and sometimes the hopelessness in their eyes. Gaining their trust wasn't easy. It took time, patience, and a willingness to simply be present. This outreach approach brought me face-to-face with the humanity beneath the diagnoses, the stories behind the symptoms. These visits, full of vulnerability and quiet despair, mirrored the emotional terrain I explored at the piano each night.

At home, the piano called me back with renewed intensity. I explored dynamics and improvisation, sharpening my sight-reading like a craftsman honing tools. Improvisation was freedom—a way to wander into unknown territory, to stay fresh, always new. That was what mattered most. Composing wasn't just a pastime—it was my reason for being. The piano became a language, a gateway to express the music stirring inside me.

Years later, I captured this feeling in a poem:

# ALWAYS NEW (THE RIVER OF INVENTION)
**6/9/2023**

*The newness*
*of the moment*
*continues*
*like a*
*winding river*
*rolling over*
*grassy terrains.*

*My musical world*
*defines itself*
*by being*
*ever present.*

*Crisp utterances*
*lay the foundation*
*for the ride to come.*

*I rejoice*
*in structures revealed,*
*in their profundity.*

In "Always New," I reflect on that ongoing freshness—the creative moment as a river flowing, ever moving, never stagnant. My work is rooted in presence—in the now. This is where music is born, one note at a time.

Those early musical gestures often set the path for a piece. There's a celebration in architecture and form, even when the direction is uncertain. Structure and mystery coexist. As composer, I live between them—attentive, listening, ready to receive.

Life's challenges and joys intertwined as I composed *Anguish in Every Household for Orchestra* (2008–10). This orchestral piece arose from personal loss and collective sorrow. The music became a vessel to hold grief—to transform it into something sharable, something others could feel and understand. In these moments, I realized creativity wasn't just self-expression—it was a bridge to others.

Life with Bill was a mix of exhilaration and unrelenting effort. He was a taskmaster, steeped in the ethic of work. Like Andy Warhol said, "All there is—is work." Productivity was identity. One day, Bill decided we'd tile every floor in the house ourselves. The project took months. Each night, I collapsed into bed—my knees sore, my joints stiffened, my energy spent.

Added to that was the daily grind of maintaining the swimming pool we'd installed. The weight of that labor pressed down on me. Then a psychiatrist friend of Bill's arrived and commandeered the Steinway for hours of jazz improvisation. Meanwhile, I juggled the house, garden, and a full-time job. I simmered in quiet frustration. Eventually, I sold the Steinway, defeated. I bought a smaller electronic keyboard instead. I had lost something precious, but I knew we were on the cusp of a new chapter. But even in defeat, a seed was germinating. Something quieter, but no less determined.

Around this time, the AIDS epidemic cast a shadow across the country. It was terrifying. A colleague from a satellite mental health office died. The virus was a silent invader. Though Bill and I were monogamous and not at risk, the fear was real. Many saw the virus as divine punishment, a cruel erasure of homosexuality. Religious zealots almost smiled at the thought. Thousands of gay men died. We survived. In surviving, we bore witness—not just to loss, but to the resilience of love.

Eventually, we flipped the Kailua house for a profit and bought a condominium in downtown Honolulu—Honolulu Park Place—on the edge of Chinatown, at Nu'uanu Avenue and Beretania Street. We lived on the top floor, in the unit originally built for the developer's daughter. The windows framed sweeping views of downtown and the harbor. It was purchased in the aftermath of the Japanese bubble crash and felt like a turning point.

In that apartment, my composition studies deepened. Bill and I grew closer—emotionally, physically. I began to gain confidence as a composer. It was there that I conceived my first CD: *Ampersand.*

After resigning from AMHD, I threw myself into serious composing. Bob Wehrman and I continued our weekly lessons. By then, I had gathered enough material for a full-length album. I hired music professors from the University of Hawai'i to perform and record my pieces.

I understood then that this would always be the way: I'd pay musicians to bring my music alive. Applying for grants felt like a waste of time. Accepting commissions? Unthinkable. I imagined the absurd stipulations: *Ten minutes, twenty seconds long, please; hire my grandson as pianist; keep it simple; deadline: high noon on December 24!* No, thank you.

It was during this fertile period that I conceived my first CD: *Ampersand* (released 2006).

It featured:

- *Piano Preludes* (2000–2001)
- *Trio for Flute, Cello, and Piano – Robust Constructs* (2005)
- *Piano Suite No. 1 for Solo Piano – The Crumb Suite* (1997–1998)
- *Frenetic Unfoldings for Solo Violin* (1998)

I released the album through my independent label, *Musica Baudino*. Commissioning Maxon Crumb to design the cover and interior artwork elevated the project. We began exchanging letters—correspondence I now treasure. Here's the text from a postcard I sent to Maxon on October 6, 2006:

*Dear Maxon,*

*I look forward to your writings and compulsive analysis. Thank you for listening—few people do. Great art is that which is irreplaceable. I find that true in your glorious expressions. Like Debussy, I have been drawn to sister art mediums for inspiration. Don't give up the energies that feed your soul. Charles Bukowski said, "If you don't gamble, you'll never win." Ampersand was that gamble—sonic vibrations among deaf ears.*

*The Unknown Composer*
*JAC*

The music, the art, the intention—they came together in harmony. *Ampersand* was my declaration—quiet, yes, but unmistakable. A birth not into fame, but into purpose.

# CHAPTER 9
## PARMA Recordings and the Professional Composer

I wasn't entirely satisfied with *Ampersand*. Back then, I was desperate to get my music "out there," but naïve about the recording process and inexperienced at guiding performers to bring out their best. As a result, the album lacks polished interpretations.

Music needs to live under your fingertips, to be fully internalized—where the instrument becomes an extension of the body. Technical mastery, physical familiarity, and expressive freedom must flow effortlessly. Instrumentalists know this fluency is second nature.

Still, the experience was valuable. I learned how vital it is to collaborate with musicians who truly understand your vision, and to communicate clearly and patiently during rehearsals. I also came to appreciate the importance of good production—how subtle choices in microphone placement, acoustics, and editing can shape the final outcome. These lessons informed every project that followed.

Maybe I should have asked Bob to produce the album. But at what cost? I'd already spent a small fortune paying musicians to interpret my work. Another bill for a producer? Not likely. I was already handing over hard-earned cash for lessons.

Aside from the mighty solo violin rendition and to hear one of the best solo piano preludes I composed at that time, *The Path is Ambiguous* (2001), *Ampersand* isn't the strongest in my catalogue. The best recordings came later, during the PARMA years.

Then an email arrived from Bob Lord, Executive Producer of PARMA Recordings in New Hampshire. He told me he'd been searching for Charles Ives online when he stumbled upon my name and listened to some recordings. He was impressed. Bob had just started a company that provided world-class performers to composers wanting their music recorded. He asked to see some of my manuscripts. I quickly sent him new works written for larger ensembles. The idea of having top-tier musicians interpret my music was thrilling—I lacked the connections to reach them myself.

Before diving into major projects, Bob, my mentor, encouraged me to study orchestral instruments deeply. Understanding each instrument's timbre, range, quirks, and whether it was transposing was crucial. This knowledge shaped my writing going forward. Better understanding of the brass section instruments, for instance, allowed me to write more effectively for the trumpet, trombone, tuba, and horn, as can be heard on *Starry Night* (2011), in the profoundly moving piece *Transcendence in the Age of War for Concert Band* (2004–2009). My string writing grew more nuanced—exploring harmonics, pizzicato, and divisi with greater purpose. This newfound understanding brought a deeper sense of color and balance to my orchestration.

This was a period of slow but steady discovery—finding my authentic voice. It wasn't a sudden epiphany, but a melody emerging from silence. *Metamorphosis 1–3* (2001) marked a personal milestone. Composed for solo viola and solo violin, these pieces explored transformation in sound and within myself—a journey toward clarity amid uncertainty.

I began the *Metamorphosis* series on March 28, 2001, eventually expanding it to include solo piano, english horn, tuba, trumpet, cello, flute, and harpsichord. Studying each instrument naturally led me to compose for larger ensembles and, eventually, the full orchestra.

*Metamorphosis No. 1 and No. 2 for Solo Viola* (2001) were recorded by Lev Zhurbin, a gifted violist and composer who leads Ljova and the Kontraband. We met through Myspace. He flew from New York to Honolulu for the sessions and gave a live performance of *Metamorphosis No. 1* at a local venue.

*Metamorphosis No. 3 (Just Do It)* (2001) for solo violin was premiered by Darel Stark on November 6, 2004, at my fiftieth birthday party, held two days after the actual date. Darel couldn't make it on the 4th, but his performance turned out to be the most unexpected gift of the evening. Hearing my music brought to life in that intimate setting—on a night filled with celebration and meaning—felt like a rite of passage. It was more than a performance; it was a quiet recognition of the path I had chosen. I remember feeling overwhelmed with gratitude, as if the universe had gently acknowledged my journey. Darel later recorded the piece, and it appears on *Music from the Ethereal Side of Paradise* (Navona Records, 2018).

Edward Gorey believed beginnings held magic. Just as *The Tale of Genji* is hailed as the first great novel, my early *Metamorphosis* works, my first orchestra piece, and first quartet hold a special place for me—full of emotional depth and expressive detail.

Through Myspace, I met other musicians: Beth Ilana Schneider-Gould, violinist; Matt Gould, guitarist (Duo46); Nathanael May, pianist; and Christian Saggese, guitarist

Duo46 and Nathanael taught in Cyprus. Their musicianship inspired me to compose a *Trio for Piano, Guitar, and Violin* (2002) and a nine-piece suite for violin and guitar titled *Romantica Passione Suite* (2004), which tells a story of romantic love and its entanglements.

Christian, born in Verona in 1974, plays classical and electric guitar and mandolin. He's won several international competitions, including First Prize at the "Andrés Segovia" International Guitar Competition in Spain. El País calls him "among the best European guitarists." I wrote *String Quintet No. 1* (2008) and *Saggese Guitar Suite (Homage to Paganini)* (2006–07) with Christian in mind. His technical mastery and passion for contemporary music made him a perfect interpreter. Christian commented on the music: "A grand formal elegance, cleanliness of thought, absolute distinctiveness. To collaborate with you is an immense pleasure." – Christian Saggese, January 8, 2007.

During the summer of 2003, I composed a series of ninety *Improvisations with Narrations for Synthesizer, Piano and Voice*. Bob, my mentor, had gone hiking in the Grand Canyon, and I used that quiet window of solitude to explore a different side of my creativity. I brought the electronic keyboard with me to Honolulu Park Place and began recording myself—improvising music and setting my own poetry to sound.

It was an opportunity to step away from classical music and immerse myself in a more accessible form of composition. At that time, I was grappling with a recurring dilemma: Do you write music that is easier to listen to and connect with, or do you write music that garners the admiration of your peers and pushes the boundaries of form? That tension has always been present.

Still, the experience of recording those improvisations was pure joy. I would turn on the recorder, begin playing freely, and recite my poetry—alive in the moment. Every recording was done in a single take, capturing the raw energy and truth of each session. I recorded one or two pieces every evening until the project was completed.

*Volere*, my second collection of solo and ensemble works, composed between 2001 and 2005, was released in 2012, a year after *Starry Night*. I wanted an album I could be proud of, without regrets over production costs. *Volere* includes *Metamorphosis No. 1 and No. 2 for Solo Viola*, two movements from *Romantica Passione Suite*, the *Trio for Piano, Guitar, and Violin, Piano Suite No. 2 for Two Pianos*, and the frenetic *Piano Suite No. 3 for Solo Piano* in five movements. Nathanael May premiered the latter in Cortona, Italy, at Teatro Signorelli Loggia on June 24, 2005. Flying to Italy for composer workshops remains one of my musical highlights.

In *Volere*'s liner notes, I wrote a three-part essay, *The Art of Creation*. I described how I start with a motif and let it evolve through editing and spontaneity. I see composers as conduits, receiving music from beyond conscious thought, embracing both the joy and sorrow of completing a work.

Under Bob's guidance, I composed enough music for PARMA's first album release of my work: *Transcendence in the Age of War* (2009). It includes my first string orchestra work, *Desiderio* (2004), which journeys through the remoteness of desire and the satisfaction of human appetites. Also featured are *Guitar Suite No. 1, Saggese Guitar Suite* (2006–07), a tribute to

Paganini and a tour de force for 6-string guitar; *String Quintet No. 1 for 10-String Guitar and String Quartet* (2008)—which reflects political divides—and *Fear of ANGST for Flute, Cello, and Piano* (2006), inspired by Bukowski's poems warning against fear-mongering.

The album's title piece, *Transcendence in the Age of War for Two Pianos* (2003) (in memory of 9/11), is a fiery lament on humanity's addiction to conflict. At the time, Bob asked, "*Where is the transcendence?*" The answer was painfully clear: There is none. You cannot transcend when war is your primary aim. Conflict fuels the ambitions of the masters of war—generals and power brokers deploying weaponry paid for by the sweat and sorrow of the American people. This piece erupts with anger and fury.

The final track, *Let Thy Mind Be Still for String Orchestra*—after a Taoist meditation by Deng Ming-Doa (2009), offers a meditative Taoist reflection, a true transcendental piece—a piece Bob once told me he wanted played at his funeral. True peace lies on the other side of the horizon.

Each work was presented with liner notes detailing its thematic intent, ranging from political tension to transcendence. The album garnered praise for its emotional depth and clarity of expression.

Henry Fogel of *Fanfare*, a magazine for record collectors that reviews hundreds of classical music releases bi-monthly, wrote:

> *"It was the final work on the disc that made the greatest impact, however, even though it lasts a mere five minutes. Let Thy Mind Be Still was inspired by a book of Taoist meditations by Deng Ming-Dao, and Carollo tells us that 'this piece speaks to the quiet stillness where peace and contentment exist and where earthly fancies are left behind.' This beautiful contemplative work could easily have a regular place in the repertoire of orchestras if conductors and administrators were aware of it. Instead of one more*

*performance of Barber's Adagio for Strings (a piece I dearly love), Let Thy Mind Be Still would resonate with listeners in a similar way, while introducing them to something new."*

PARMA went on to release several more albums: *Starry Night* (2011), *The Transfiguration of Giovanni Baudino* (2017, PARMA's 500th release), *Music from the Ethereal Side of Paradise* (2018), and *Symphony No. 3* (2019).

Of these, *Starry Night* is my favorite. I initially hesitated to fund another all-Carollo album, but Bob insisted it was important. I financed it myself. The result was deeply rewarding. *Starry Night for String Orchestra*—after Van Gogh's *Starry Night Over the Rhône* (1888), Musée d'Orsay, Paris (2009)—stands as one of my most evocative works.

One reviewer wrote:

*"The disc takes its title from the first piece, Starry Night for String Orchestra. Brilliantly and inventively written, the piece dwells on the 'fear of the unknown.' This vital composition is captured in close, involving sound."*

*Starry Night* also includes my first orchestral composition: *Anguish in Every Household* (2008–10).

Gapplegate had this to say about it:

*"The orchestral piece 'Anguish in Every Household' fits in with these two in that all three have something of the crusty pioneers of American modernism—Ives, Ruggles and perhaps Henry Brant—embedded in them. (And others, too.) The thought is that he roots himself in the past in order to create another possible future for American classical music."*

*Transcendence in the Age of War for Concert Band* (2004–09) (in memory of 9/11) is perhaps my most ambitious—blending development with wit, it remains my most impassioned artistic statement. Colin Clarke, *Fanfare* music critic, declared, "One of the composer's most emotionally powerful utterances, it deserves a place in the repertoire."

I dedicated *Quartet No. 1 for Clarinet, Violin, Cello, and Piano (A Worded Grey Enigma)* (2000) to Edward Gorey. Immersed in his universe—his books, dolls, intricate illustrations—I used Gorey quotes as movement titles. He died before hearing the music, which saddened me deeply. I later learned he had declined a recommended medical procedure. After his death, I felt robbed of his unique genius. No more pen-and-ink drawings to satisfy that mysterious hunger inside me.

I donated much of my John A. Carollo–Edward Gorey Collection to the Hamilton Library at the University of Hawai'i at Manoa, hoping future readers and artists find inspiration in his strange vision.

In 2010, the art museum organized a major exhibition drawn from my extensive donation. Serving as a docent for the exhibit was one of the true highlights of my life, as I knew the backstories behind many of the objects on display. Meeting Andreas Brown, the legendary proprietor of the Gotham Book Mart, was both an honor and a delight. He served as a special guest speaker for one of the many events hosted during that period, which also included a panel discussion, theatrical performance, and illustration workshops. The following year, *Looking for Edward Gorey* was published—a richly detailed volume now considered a classic exploration of Gorey's unique art and vision. It includes a thoughtful, detailed essay by Joseph Stanton on Edward's whimsical and haunting visual world.

In 2022, I wrote an essay, *Compositional Features Found in Edward Gorey's Works*, exploring how his rhythmic visual style and layered textures mirror musical structure and development. Music and Gorey's narratives both move audiences forward—frame by frame, phrase by phrase.

Finally, *Nothing Shall Come of This for String Orchestra (A Lament for Unheard Music)* (2009) speaks to the quiet despair of creating something with care and conviction—only to have it languish, unseen, unplayed, unheard.

*Starry Night* received glowing reviews. MusicWeb International's Byzantion wrote:

> *"Thankfully, Navona Records have rescued these superb works from total obscurity, giving at least those who are prepared to look hard enough the opportunity to discover new music that often has every right to stand alongside the great works of past centuries..."*

Colin Clarke from *Fanfare* had this to say:

> *"Previously, I enjoyed John A. Carollo's disc, The Transfiguration of Giovanni Baudino (Fanfare 41:3), and a disc including Desiderio and Transcendence in the Age of War (Fanfare 41:5). This newest disc further confirms Carollo as a major compositional voice, while also offering the concert band version of Transcendence."*

*The Transfiguration of Giovanni Baudino* (2017), *Music from the Ethereal Side of Paradise* (2018), and *Symphony No. 3* (2019) also earned excellent reviews. Flying to London for the *Symphony No. 3* recording was a career highlight. Working with the London Symphony Orchestra humbled and affirmed me.

My only gripe with PARMA was that my music was sometimes recorded before live performances. Hearing a piece live first allows the composer, performers, and audience to feel its shape. I might realize a passage needs adjustment, a tempo shift, or a texture change. Rehearsals and concerts often spark breakthroughs—small tweaks that clarify the music. Sometimes, minor revisions after hearing a live premiere make all the difference. This practice allows for a dialogue between composers and executants and allows musicians to get the music "under the fingertips"—the music internalized in their muscle memory, physical movements becoming second nature.

Most of my PARMA recordings came before my move to Portland in 2018. Working with musicians in Hawaiʻi was challenging; a good deal of gifted musicians were on the mainland. Still, PARMA published full albums and featured my pieces on many compilations.

One highlight was *Abrazo*, recorded in Cuba, where I met Cuba's greatest trumpeter and a fine guitarist who recorded my *Burlesque for Trumpet in B-flat and Classical Guitar* (2007). The experience was unlike any other—infused with a sense of cultural exchange and emotional immediacy. The musicians' curiosity and openness created a collaborative atmosphere that felt raw and real. Answering their questions about the music wasn't just gratifying—it felt like a shared act of discovery, of breathing life into the notes in a way that transcended borders. *Abrazo* was released June 10, 2016.

*Burlesque* tells the story of Rosa, who encounters two musicians playing strange instruments—a trumpet and a guitar. She starts dancing wildly, captivated. Luca, the trumpet player, plays a bold cadenza to impress her. Rosa discovers life can be strange but beautiful when played well. The finale sees her lying on stage, embracing Luca's trumpet, smiling with contentment.

Reviews praised *Burlesque*: "John A. Carollo's *Burlesque* is a tour de force duet for the unlikely pairing of Fadev Sanjudo Rodríguez's trumpet and Merlyn de la Caridad Corona Pérez's guitar. The composition is immensely original and intriguing, especially in the context of an album focused on jazz."

Another work that evolved in a deeply personal way was *Piano Étude No. 14 – Histories II* (2007) (The full score is provided separately at the end of the memoir). I dedicated this piece to Hugh Sung, an accomplished pianist working for The Curtis Institute for Music. It began as a quiet meditation on lineage and transmission—on the ancient, intimate act of passing on touch, tone, and musical understanding.

Written as part of a lineage of études, *Histories II* honors the invisible line that runs from teacher to student, from composer to performer, from past to present.

Marked "Delicate with Beauty of Tone," it opens like a whisper—chromatic threads spinning above a subtle left-hand grounding. Grace notes, played just before the beat, evoke the elegance of eras gone by, when mastery was felt in the breath between notes. As the piece unfolds, rhythmic complexity builds: cascading 32nd-note patterns, accelerating triplets, and dense voicings create both turbulence and motion. But like memory, the étude returns. "Come primo" leads us back to the origin—the quiet space where music first awakened. Here, technique is a doorway to remembrance.

Years later, I transcribed the étude for piano and orchestra with the title *Passing on Ancient Skills for Piano and Orchestra* (2024)—a transformation that gave it sweeping emotional breadth without losing its meditative core. This version was recorded by the Royal Scottish National Orchestra. PARMA Recordings released it along with other musical contributions on August 8, 2025. It won a Silver Medal award from the Global Music Awards shortly thereafter.

This orchestral realization stands as a testament to the evolving life of my music—how a single gesture, first written in solitude, can be reborn through larger forces and shared anew.

Two PARMA contracts gave me the extraordinary honor of premieres at Carnegie Hall. Flying to New York with friends to attend was unforgettable. Sitting inside Weill Recital Hall, Carnegie's intimate space, felt surreal. Soft gold walls, ornate moldings, a glittering chandelier—everything breathed quiet grandeur. Rows of red velvet seats faced a warmly lit stage where every sound shimmered.

I wondered how many composers before me had waited in that very spot, hearts pounding, hoping their music would be heard. The hall held echoes of their dreams and triumphs. What an honor to be part of that lineage, hearing my music come alive in such a revered place, embraced by listeners.

Another honor was winning Silver at the Global Music Awards for Piano Etude No. II "Sightless," featured on PARMA's *Pinnacle Vol. 2*. This recognition wouldn't have happened without PARMA's promotion and belief in the quality of my music.

After thirteen and a half years, my composition lessons with Bob ended. He was proud of my growth but lamented I hadn't learned sight-singing earlier—a skill best absorbed young. Still, my inner ear was strong, and I composed fluently. I had arrived. I could compose confidently for full orchestra, and the muse was always nearby.

Being an outsider had its advantages:

- I created music unbound by tradition, honoring the independence that defined my journey.
- I followed my own rules, trusting the instincts honed in solitude and persistence.
- I no longer needed to "find my voice"—it lived in the moment, born of countless private awakenings.
- I resisted crowd mentality, choosing clarity of purpose over convention.
- My music remained fresh, vital, and unmistakably mine.

As years passed, my works became less isolated pieces and more extensions of myself. *Symphony No. 5 – Classic Beauty Over Surface Novelty* (2022–23) represents this maturity—a blend of tradition and innovation, a conversation with my own artistic legacy. It asks what endures beyond applause—what remains when the echoes fade.

# CHAPTER 10

## The Big Island: Renewal and the Return of Giovanni

*"We are the music-makers, And we are the dreamers of dreams."*
– Arthur O'Shaughnessy

*"To listen is to hear the musical diary of my life."*
– JAC

Bill died on March 8, 2014, just three months after we were married (December 2, 2013), and our union was finally recognized by law. It was a profoundly difficult time. I felt utterly alone, with few to share my days or dreams with. Deep grief shattered both my heart and health. Even the mere mention of his name could bring me to tears. That intensity lasted about a year, though the sorrow lingered for at least three more.

I recalled all the good times we shared and the projects we built together—each one deepening our bond and reminding me how we thrived side by side. One of our first acts of care was convincing Bill to quit smoking shortly after we met—a symbol of the life we were creating.

My career path in mental health services with the Adult Mental Health Division/Department of Health could not have happened without Bill's support. In the evenings, we often strategized about how to address the issues and challenges I faced in my various government roles.

During my time as a social worker at HSH, I received an ACE Award (Achievements in Civil Excellence) from the State of Hawai'i. Bill was instrumental in reviewing the proposal I sent to the state and giving advice. The recognition came after I discovered that paying Medicare premiums for indigent HSH patients would ultimately save the State significant funds when patients were administratively discharged from HSH for medical procedures and then returned.

While music filled my inner world, I also found meaning in pragmatic solutions—proof that art and logic can live side by side.

One of our happiest moments was receiving a Civil Union granted by the State of Hawai'i on January 5, 2012. Bill wasn't one for celebration or ceremony, but the photo of us draped in leis, faces beaming with joy, remains a cherished memory. Another highlight was our trip to the Grand Canyon. The vast rock formations—ancient and immense—left us in awe, standing as timeless monuments, silent witnesses to enduring love.

Bill's death recalled my adopted father's passing—painful but for different reasons. I had cared for Dad during his last five years. Flying to Rome, New York, to help him pack and sell his belongings stirred memories of our time in Oil City. I decided to bring Dad to Honolulu, into the home Bill and I had built together, after receiving a letter from him that simply said, "I love you." It was the first time he had ever said those words. In that moment, I felt truly loved and knew he cared. I could not let him fade away alone in a shabby apartment.

From this poignant time, I learned a hard truth: Don't wait to tell people you love them. Time is uncertain. Relationships can fracture or vanish. Unspoken love turns into regret. The people we care for most are not guaranteed tomorrow. Expressing love—plainly, directly—is one of the few ways we heal wounds, bridge silence, and bring light into another's darkness.

*Love held back becomes sorrow. Love unspoken becomes silence. And silence, over time, becomes a wound.*

I saw this in Bill's anguish and in my father's breakthrough to say those simple words.

Back in Honolulu, I tended to Dad's every need—doctor's visits, daily care, even walks to the local Roman Catholic Church. Those walks stirred mixed feelings. As a child, I hadn't realized I was just a case number, an infant available for adoption. Yet accompanying Dad to that church gave me a quiet satisfaction, a connection I hadn't felt before. Tony was happy, reunited at last with his adopted son. Over time, he came to understand the value of relationships—gay ones included—and that acceptance brought us both some peace.

Eventually, I found comfort in music again. I bought a Sauter Upright German Piano. The key aspect of Sauter's reputation is its use of only German-made parts, ensuring high quality and adherence to traditional craftsmanship. A lovely piano, I enjoyed hours and hours of playing the intermediate music I could accomplish without too many mistakes!

Composing a suite for one of my favorite ensembles, the string orchestra, was a breeze. *The Rhetoric and Mythos of Belief* (2014) was for Bill, composed not long after his passing, to express the profound sorrow of losing a lifelong partner. The movements are:

- Part I – *Profondo*
- Part II – *Animato – Largo*
- Part III – *Tranquillo (Existential Loneliness, as a background for joy and sorrow)*

- Part IV – *Misterioso / Meditativo (Bill's Memorial Piece – Your Heart Rests Within Mine)*
- Part V – *Intenso*

This is one of the finest works on the PARMA Recordings release *The Transfiguration of Giovanni Baudino* (2017). Also included on this all-Carollo album:

- *Let Freedom Ring for Orchestra* (2015)
- *Do You Have an E.R. for Music? for Orchestra* (2012)
- *The Transfiguration of Giovanni Baudino for Piano and Orchestra* (2008–2010)
- *Symphony No. 2 (The Circle of Fire)* (2013)
- *Move Towards the Light (Your Destiny Awaits You) for String Orchestra* (2015)

Music critic Greg Applegate Edwards wrote in *Gapplegate Classical-Modern Music Review:* "The works have great forward rhythmic momentum without following a 'Rites' model—or any other in any obvious way. The music is consequential and enlivening. It exists in its own singular category as Carollo music. That is saying a great deal."

That phrase struck a deep chord. It captured what I have always hoped to offer: Music that not only moves forward with intent but also moves the listener inward, toward aliveness.

I later wrote a poem inspired by those words:

## MUSIC SHOULD BE CONSEQUENTIAL AND ENLIVENING

*each note a ripple*
*each sentence a wave*

*cast into silence*
*cast into light*

*each silence a breath*
*each utterance breathing*

*held open by wonder*
*held open by splendor*

*born of longing*
*born of solitude*

*it listens before it speaks*
*then speaks with conviction*

*by the urgency of beauty*
*by the urgency of love*

*love for the craft*
*love for awakening*

*music for remembrance*
*music for reverence of beauty*

This is my goal: not merely to compose, but to stir, to awaken, to transform. The music must mean something. It must be born of silence and destined for presence.

## *Program Notes for the Transfiguration of Giovanni Baudino for Piano and Orchestra*

This work was transcribed from *Piano Étude No. 6 – Incystence* (2005). At the time, a few friends were suffering from medical ailments, and I dedicated several études to them to lift their spirits. I have always been fascinated by metamorphosis—the idea that nothing in nature is static. Musically, I strive to translate this sense of change by composing works that evolve so that no two musical moments are ever identical. In *The Transfiguration of Giovanni Baudino*, we witness how a person's life transforms over time. Since everything is new, we are—as we once were—as fresh as a meandering stream rolling over ever-changing landscapes. Pedal markings for piano and celesta serve as guides only. My aesthetic calls for interpretation on the performer's part. Dynamic markings are suggestions, though they should work well as written. – JAC

## *Liner Notes for the CD Release: The Transfiguration of Giovanni Baudino*

Everything is new. I've always preferred to let music speak for itself. Each listener derives unique meanings from their experience, most of them felt viscerally. For me, music should reflect the newness of the day. At its best, it is fresh and alive, embodying the moment, which is always unique. There are no two identical moments in nature. Like a river meandering through dynamic landscapes, music should evolve over time, offering newness in motion. This concept of metamorphosis fascinates me, along with the truth that nothing in nature is static. My music seeks to embody that.

In my development as a composer, being crisp and concise has become a conscious priority—taking a simple idea and unfolding it with care. Reflecting on my poetry, I realize the most effective poems focus on a single idea. Simplicity is the most difficult thing to express. You can hear this most profoundly in my string orchestra works. These pieces are tightly composed, reflecting the day-to-day realities of life—its humor, demands, joys, and sorrows. Whether exploring the ironic need for a musical emergency room (*Do You Have an E.R. for Music?*) or the human journey of transformation (*The Transfiguration of Giovanni Baudino*), these works are musical portraits of lived experience—vivid, emotional, and deeply alive. — JAC

Pleased with the release—especially as it marked PARMA's 500th—I proposed a special vinyl edition, my first LP. I hired Alex Gross, a visual artist known for his oil paintings exploring globalization, consumerism, beauty, and dystopia, to create the cover art. That painting now hangs proudly in the hallway of my Portland apartment.

What did The *Transfiguration of Giovanni Baudino* mean to me?

It was not just another composition—it was an invocation, a ceremony, a rite of return. In giving musical voice to the name I was born with, I reclaimed a part of myself that had long been silenced. Giovanni Baudino was the boy erased by paperwork, sent across an ocean, renamed, and forgotten by the systems that facilitated his disappearance.

*This piece was my way of saying: I remember him. I am him.*

*Cover for The Transfiguration of Giovanni Baudino. Art by Alex Gross*

To transfigure something is not merely to change it—but to elevate it, to reveal its sacred essence. In this orchestral work, I sought to raise my origin story out of obscurity and into sound. The piano, tender and exposed, became the voice of that lost child. The orchestra became the emotional landscape of a journey—from abandonment to awareness, from secrecy to self-recognition. It was a personal resurrection through music. I wasn't just writing a score—I was restoring identity. Transforming memory. Honoring the mystery of how someone survives silence and becomes whole through sound. For all the children like me, whose names were lost and found again, *The Transfiguration of Giovanni Baudino* is a testimony: The past does not vanish. It waits—for music, for love, for the courage to speak.

The title, *The Transfiguration of Giovanni Baudino*, is itself a declaration. It points to something more than transformation—it suggests a radiant revealing. "Giovanni Baudino" was the name I was born with but never called. To use it in the title is to give it light, breath, and sound. This work is not simply autobiographical—it is symbolic. It marks the lifting of that name out of historical silence and into an audible, visible presence. In writing this piece, I reclaimed my origins and reshaped them through art. It is not about erasing pain but about illuminating it—so that beauty might emerge from its shadow.

I also had time for other works:

- *Sextet for Clarinet in B-flat, Horn in F, Tuba, Piano and Cello (How Many Times?)* (2016–17)
- *The Iron Cage of Reason for Solo Piano* (2017)
- *Awakenings (Orchestral Suite II)* (2015–16), inspired by my poem of the same name
- *Symphony No. 3* (2017)

- *Music from the Ethereal Side of Paradise for Chamber Orchestra* (2017)
- *Appeasement and Containment for Concert Band (The Lies Fly By)* (2018)

I've collected Alex Gross's works for years. His brand of American pop surrealism portrays a world teetering on the edge—oversaturated with marketing, overwhelmed by industry, and spiritually starved by excess. His characters walk city streets emblazoned with corporate logos, numb to their absurd surroundings. His art, at once ironic and unsettling, hangs near my Edward Gorey originals, prints, drawings, and other Goreyana along a long hallway in my downtown Portland apartment—a city alive with artists, musicians, readers, and protestors. It's all here.

Back in Honolulu, some friends urged me to move to the Big Island. Their reasons were unclear, their motives even more so. But I agreed, thinking a change might do me good. Life there was peaceful; the landscapes breathtaking. I continued to compose, finishing *Let Freedom Ring for Orchestra* (2015) and *The Rhetoric and Mythos of Belief for String Orchestra* (2014).

The talented Italian guitarist Christian Sagesse visited and recorded several solo guitar pieces that made up enough material for an EP released by my label, Musica Baudino. *Saggese Plays Carollo* is now available on streaming services.

I became friendly with a man who had worked on my new townhouse in the resort community of Mauna Lani. He looked at me with seductive eyes. A three-year affair began. This isolated enclave was mostly populated by affluent mainlanders who visited their properties once or twice a year. Watering landscaping for my "friends" who persuaded me to move grew tiresome. Eventually, I left Mauna Lani—hot, mosquito-ridden, and expensive—and moved into a newly built home in Waikoloa Village, cooler and up in the hills.

The affair continued, providing stress relief during a time when I was still grappling with Bill's loss. He said his marriage left emotional needs unmet—needs I could fulfill. But guilt overtook me.

We came from opposite ends of the political spectrum. Watching him walk into my bedroom felt like a betrayal—not only of Bill but of myself. How could anyone find comfort in talk shows spewing hate-filled lies and propaganda? I tried to convince myself that kindness remained a virtue. Generosity, consideration, and compassion are traits I admired.

I will say this: I loved gardening. Landscaping the Waikoloa house brought me joy and balance—a retreat from composing, lust, and grief. A doctor in Honolulu once told me I had "found the best of all worlds." But I wasn't so sure.

I made a list—reasons to stay, reasons to leave—and when I was done, I called my real estate agent. "Sell the house," I said. "I'm moving to Portland."

I chose Portland for its thriving art and music scene, a place where creativity breathes in the streets. But the decision was also practical—climate change had made Hawai'i unbearably hot and humid. Locals never needed ceiling fans in every room fifty years ago... It was time to find a climate that matched both my body and my spirit. And so, I went north—drawn by necessity, and the promise of something more: a life renewed in sound.

# CHAPTER 11

## Portland Bound

Bags packed, container loaded, suitcases in the car—the trip to the airport felt surreal. I reflected on the twenty-nine years I'd spent in Hawai'i. Leaving once again, stepping into the unknown, had become a familiar theme in my life. Brion Gysin's *Here to Go* felt especially fitting. Later, I would compose a piano work bearing that very name.

My close companion cried as we said goodbye. I hadn't realized the depth of his concern until that moment. "I had no idea," I told him. Still, I knew I was doing the right thing. Leaving for another land meant acknowledging that the affair had run its course. I was also saying farewell to a small circle of gay friends I had just begun to know. We had shared meals and card games, warmed by the Hawaiian breeze and the stillness of endless vistas.

Two months earlier, I'd visited Portland to search for a new home, hoping to transfer the equity from my Waikoloa house. The final property shown to me was in a 1922 Victorian building. I immediately fell in love with its high ceilings, picture rail moldings in every room, and the ornate structure framing nine floors of historic condominiums.

When the moving truck arrived carrying the full weight of my household, I took stock of everything. Over the following weeks, I opened one box at a time, reacquainting myself with the curated life I'd built—books, vinyl records, and CDs; stamps and postcards; comic books and graphic novels; Goreyana; and original artwork and prints collected over many years.

Among the artwork were four delicate watercolors of flowers that once grew near the Ira Floyd House in National City, CA, back when it was a farm more than 120 years ago. They'd been painted by Carrie Harbison, the builder's daughter. Carrie's son, Charles Harbison, had gifted them to Bill and me as a housewarming present when we moved into the Floyd House. He told us many of her works were housed in the National City Library. A few years later, I wrote to the library, offering the four paintings to complete their collection. Their enthusiastic response confirmed that I'd made the right decision. The paintings were sent and now form part of their Floyd holdings.

This donation reminded me of a sale I made to the Northwestern University Library. In 1998, I purchased a letter from Larry Moskowitz of Loblolly Books in Los Angeles—a long-lost correspondence from Pierre Boulez to John Cage, in which Boulez outlined the basis of his serial theory. Somehow, this letter had never made it into the John Cage archives at Northwestern. In Joan Peyser's *Boulez: Composer, Conductor, Enigma* (Schirmer Books, 1976), the letter is mentioned briefly, with an image of the final page I recognized instantly since I held the original.

On February 29, 2012, I contacted the Northwestern Library and informed them that I had the missing letter. As a collector, I understand the value of completeness—how one missing piece can shift our understanding of a larger narrative. Just as I had done with my Edward Gorey archive—donating over 1,900 items to the University of Hawai'i at Manoa to establish the John A. Carollo–Edward Gorey Collection—I wanted to ensure the Boulez-Cage letter was returned to its rightful home.

This "completist" instinct has shaped much of my life. Whether collecting, composing, or simply living, I've always sought the satisfaction of seeing things through to the end. Hundreds of scores completed. Dozens of projects resolved. The work may be demanding, but reaching the finish line is exhilarating, rewarding—and, yes, fun.

With everything in its place, I returned to music. A set of solo piano pieces titled *Phantasmamusica* began to take shape in 2019. I envisioned it as an ongoing series of fantastic, inventive musical creations. Each book would contain nine pieces—my favorite number and a number that creeps into my music—and one that had drawn me since early composition lessons. The name *Phantasmamusica* comes from "phantasmagoria," a sequence of dreamlike or surreal images. Slightly altered, it perfectly captured my aesthetic.

I also thought of "phantasmagory," referring to A.M. Stephens' dark nursery rhymes and vintage art, and *Phantasmagorey*, the title of a 1974 Yale exhibit catalogue on Edward Gorey, created by Clifford Ross and Dale R. Roylance. These references felt kindred to my musical vision. So far, I've completed six books, each containing nine pieces. Only the most accomplished pianists can take on this challenge. Some material in Book 6 is currently being transformed into my Sixth Symphony.

Since moving to Portland, musical works have flowed freely (a selection):

- *The Nomadic Composer* for Clarinet in B-flat, Bassoon, Piano, Violin, and Cello (2018)
- *Humoresque* for Guitar and Small Orchestra (2018)

- *Orchestra Concerto: Longinus, On Sublimity* (2019)
- *Symphony No. 4* (2020)
- *Hello Thanatos, Eros Calling* (Orchestral Suite III) (2020–21)
- *Phantasmamusica* for Solo Piano, Books I-VI (2021–2025)
- *Symphony No. 5: Classic Beauty Over Surface Novelty (Terminal Originality)* (2022–23)
- *Funeral Dirge: Permanence in Change* for Orchestra (2023)
- *Passing on Ancient Skills* for Piano and Orchestra (2024)
- *Symphony No. 6: Everything is Connected* (2025–26), a work in progress

After reading poems in *The Essential Goethe,* edited by Matthew Bell and published by Princeton University Press, I composed *Music for Choir and Orchestra* (2019–20). I felt a kinship with Goethe's deep understanding of love, nature, and the unknown. For example, in his poem "The Godlike" (early 1780s), the line "Hail to the unknown"—within broader themes of moral action and choosing between good and evil—is written with a rhythmic urgency, a forward momentum you'll discover in my own music. Setting his poetry came easily, as if I channeled his energies through me into the black and white notations we call music.

Other choral works followed: *Dark Days for Choir and Orchestra* (2020) and *Artistic Ideals for Choir and Large Ensemble* (2021).

Setting text from my own poems, *Music for Choir* (2012) was both personal and rewarding. This choral setting, dedicated to Bill for unaccompanied choir, was a joy I can hardly describe.

One of them, *Little Gems,* has since been performed worldwide.

Two pieces from the song cycle *Exhortation! For Voice, Piano and Violin* (1999; revised 2013) premiered in Honolulu in 2001 by the Stark Duo. I selected the poems for *Exhortation!* after reading hundreds by Bukowski. I enjoyed his work so deeply that I began collecting signed first editions. Years later, I sold them all to a collector in Los Angeles for over $40,000. Recovering my investment, I poured the money into my true passion: music—paying musicians to understand, perform, and record my compositions.

William Blake's mystical reverence for nature, imagination, and innocence stirred something deep in me. His poems opened windows into the eternal, the visionary. I was moved to compose a song cycle titled *Awake Humanity to Nature's Beauty!* (2007)—a series of musical settings tracing an arc from wonder to revelation (the violin version premiered on Hawai'i PBS Radio Station on August 25, 2012, featuring the Stark Duo).

I also collaborated with Andrea Hollander, a poet I met in my building. Her poetry inspired *Transcendence After Loss* for Choir, Piano, Harp, Horn in F, Tuba, and Cello (2020).

Over the years, critical recognition grew. Reviewers appreciated the depth, originality, and expressive power of my music. I was proud of the thoughtful praise after each release. Their words reminded me that, though composing is often solitary, music can—and does—resonate deeply with others.

Receiving reviews was never the goal, but they affirmed something deeply personal—that my music was being heard, felt, and understood. Each line of praise reminded me I wasn't composing into a void. In a world that often overlooks quiet creation, these voices echoed back a connection. They showed that what I wrote in solitude could resonate across time and place. That, in itself, felt like belonging.

I bought a Mason & Hamlin Grand Piano, known for its robust construction. The Artist series provides a big sound that the upright could not provide. Jim Paul would have been proud of me, swearing that they were one of the best instruments made, with warm sound, powerful bass, and clear treble.

Then came 2022—a year I'll always remember. I met David Greger online through Match.com. I was in Italy, visiting Lorenzo and Giusy for the first time, when he replied to my message. I suggested we meet for coffee upon my return. We met at Umbria Caffè in Portland's Pearl District. I found him clever, bright, humorous, talented (he plays violin), engaging, and a joy to be with. He had deep musical connections in Portland, a place he'd cultivated all his life.

As Vice President of Chamber Music Northwest, perhaps he could open doors for me, I thought. But the truth is, no doors needed opening. I had already lived a rich life of music making—one that has been deeply satisfying and rewarding on its own terms.

Finding David (and Lorenzo and Giusy around the same time) was not only the fermata over a life's worth of sound, but the final chord that continues to resonate.

And the music goes on, quietly, in the heart.

# CHAPTER 12

## The Music of Words: Selected Poems and Reflections

### Abstract

This chapter presents a recital in words, where poetry and music converge as dialects of the same inner language. Across its movements—dream and imagination, creation and process, transformation and transcendence, nature and awe, grief and connection, struggle and irony—each poem reveals the composer's private dialogue with mystery, silence, and sound. Some pieces rise with joy; others sting with satire; others ache with loss; yet all belong to the same current of artistic necessity. Read together, they form not a collection of isolated works but a suite: a journey through the thresholds of the creative spirit, affirming that *art does not ask for permission to exist—it insists on being.*

# OVERTURE

*Between silence and sound,*
*a line is drawn—*
*not by hand,*
*but by breath,*
*by dream,*
*by pulse.*

*Poetry leans toward music,*
*music leans toward poetry,*
*and in their leaning*
*they become one.*

*Here begins a recital*
*of the inner life—*
*verses and tones*
*woven together,*
*singing what words alone*
*cannot hold.*

In my world, *music and poetry are inseparable.* Each feeds the other. Poetry gives me focus and tone for the music I compose, and music, in turn, gives voice to the silence between words. I have placed this chapter here, near the memoir's end, because poetry—like music—offers an intimate glimpse into my inner life. These are sketches of thought, fragments of dream, and philosophical reflections shaped across decades of composing. In them, you will find the same energy that animates my scores—the pulse of longing, the surprise of transformation, the urgency of creation. This chapter is a companion suite to my musical life.

## Dream & Imagination

Imagination is the wellspring of creativity, where identity and art blur into one. In "Into the Zone of a Dream," I enter that fertile realm where the artist dissolves into the very art that reveals the soul. The original poem was part of my extensive *Crafted Stardust, Improvisations with Narrations for Synthesizer, Piano, and Voice* (2003), where shifting electronic timbres echoed the ethereal nature of dreams.

Similarly, "Express Your Dream" speaks with the fearless voice of youth—the urgency to give fleeting thoughts form before they vanish, the innocence to risk creation without hesitation.

"Imaginative Poets" turns inward to the compulsion that drives us: the irresistible need to shape words and music into something that transcends the self, inviting others to share the bloodstream of imagination.

And in "Take Me to No. 9 Heaven," I offer a vision of artistic paradise: a transcendent place where music and nature converge in harmony, and where the composer's spirit finds eternal rest in creation itself.

## 1. INTO THE ZONE OF A DREAM
### (Revised text, original text set to music)

*Escape into the dream zone,*
*dissolve into invisible steam.*
*Become the art*
*that reveals your soul.*

*Reflect, envision, live—*

*a dreamer to some,*
*a vision to yourself.*

## 2. EXPRESS YOUR DREAM
### (Text set to music)

*Express your dream on a stage,*
*Be an innocent youth without age,*

*Fly on the edge of a sensation,*
*Send a fanciful thought narration,*

*Know the reason of a fond hope,*
*Ride the thin line of a slope,*

*Have the courage to see a plea,*
*Pass through a mind carefree,*

*Caress the image passing by,*
*Sense the vision of my eye.*

## 3. IMAGINATIVE POETS
### (Revised text, original text set to music)

*Imaginative poets*
*must dream,*

*shape words into sculpture,*

*open a world*
*inside a bubble's surface,*

*or stretch your horizon*
*beyond its frame.*

*They live within the dream,*
*inviting you*
*into their bloodstream.*

## 4. TAKE ME TO NO. 9 HEAVEN
### (Text set to music)

*Take me to No. 9 heaven*

*where scented flowers fill manicured gardens,*
*where glorious trumpets sound notes triumphantly,*
*where sparkling waterfalls flow down steep mountain slopes,*
*where no signs of human existence can be seen,*
*where trees harbor plentiful exotic yellow and white birds,*
*where daily rainbows blanket crystal-clear landscapes,*
*and where I can experience eternal peace composing*

## *Creation & Process*

Composing music is a sculptural act, blending intention with intuition to uncover originality. To me, music is necessity, not decoration—a language that reveals the soul of its maker.

In "The Essence of His Being," the musician becomes sculptor, chiseling sound from an inner palette of colors and textures until identity itself takes audible form.

At times, the work resists control, as if guided by its own unseen momentum. In "Music Writes Itself," the composer marvels at how the music transcends its maker, carrying both listener and creator toward a divine conclusion.

Other pieces grow quietly, like seeds nurtured by solitude and patience. "Like the Whispering of the Wind" reflects this emergence—phrases that appear like soft utterances, gradually shaping themselves in stillness.

I have long trusted the vitality of first drafts. They may be flawed, but they carry the spark of surprise. "Advice on Musical Drafts" is a reminder to honor spontaneity, for the unexpected often leads to astonishment and joy.

I honor the invisible work of shaping sound in "Scaffolding," where temporary frameworks support a music that ultimately breathes on its own. Beneath structure lies mystery, however, and I have often felt myself less architect than conduit. "It Came from the Ether" affirms this sense: music arrives not from intellect but from beyond, flowing through the composer who listens and translates.

This vision deepens in "Conduits," where every artist is a vessel of larger forces, bridging the seen and unseen, the temporal and the eternal.

## 5. THE ESSENCE OF HIS BEING

*The musician sculptures*
*his masterpiece*
*from within his personal musical language.*

*He erects a wall of sound*
*unique to his palette*
*of harmonic colors and textures.*

*Chiseling forms recognizable to himself,*
*he satisfies his inner ear.*

*These daily rations fulfill a need,*
*an insatiable appetite for sonic worlds,*
*capturing the essence of his being.*

## 6. MUSIC WRITES ITSELF

*After the first few musical ideas*
*the music begins to have a life of its own.*

*It's as if the presentation had momentum*
*thrusting itself forward into a rich sonic world.*

*The composer molds his creation*
*into a shapely form anew.*

*Splendid in its articulation,*
*profound in its style,*
*the music traverses a mutation*
*of rhythmically charged motives.*

*On its way to a divine conclusion,*
*you are left speechless,*
*moved, and transported,*
*to a new dimension.*

*Mood elevated,*
*fixed on the present,*
*you are profoundly changed,*
*and pleased.*

*You marvel at its beauty.*

# 7. LIKE THE WHISPERING OF THE WIND

*Using the seed of an idea,*
*carving away in solitude,*
*amorphous possibilities take form.*

*Musical phrases speak*
*in soft utterances,*
*slowly,*
*as time stands still.*

*Sonic gestures*
*from morning to sunset*
*grace the pages of my music,*
*revealing beauty*
*within the ethereal side of Paradise.*

# 8. ADVICE ON MUSICAL DRAFTS

*As you begin to compose,*
*the first draft becomes an impression;*

*often flawed,*
*but full of promise.*

*It's the editing process that brings the music to life.*

*When you do not know where the music will lead you,*
*then surprises and astonishments await.*

*Wonderment and joy are the final result,*
*as your journey to perfection satisfies.*

*Trust your senses,*
*spontaneity is the key component to originality.*

## 9. SCAFFOLDING

**(Revised text, original text set to music)**

*We raise walls of sound*
*on scaffolds of tone,*
*chiseling pitches*
*into harmonic form.*

*The muse nods—*
*structures emerge,*
*suspended on hooks*
*for the ear's judgment.*

*The composer discards banality,*
*weaves voices into joy.*

*The scaffolds fall away,*
*leaving the structure—*
*profound,*
*breathless.*

## 10. IT CAME FROM THE ETHER

*People ask,*
*"John, where does your music come from?"*
*I reply,*
*"From the ether."*

*The music has always been there.*
*I am the medium that gives it expression;*
*The conduit between the mystical realms.*

*The intermediate communicating a musical language;*
*The dream poet expressing musical facts.*

*A channel conveying meaning to notational values;*
*A fountain that flows from the ether to your ears.*

## 11. CONDUITS
### (Revised text, original text set to music)

*We are conduits,*

*vehicles to another world*
*of bliss and ecstasy,*

*absorbing events*
*for the future,*
*fulfilling destiny—*
*a star among billions,*
*burning in the heavens.*

## *Transformation & Transcendence*

Music has the power to lift us beyond ourselves. It transforms burdens into possibility reshaping spirit and perception.

In "Metamorphosis No. 9," shifting patterns ascend like rivers through varied terrain, lifting the listener to a new dimension, renewing vitality, and reminding us that change is always possible.

"Moon Dust" evokes our cosmic inheritance, where ancestral presence and celestial matter intermingle. It is both intimate and infinite—an image of how we carry within us the touch of those who came before.

In "Crafted Stardust," I meditate on our shared origins. We are fragments of a greater whole, sculptors and sculptures at once, carving meaning from the raw material of existence, applauded by the quiet recognition of connection.

"Millennium Loops" continues this vision through sound: hums, buzzes, surreal transformations, and temporal play. It is a dreamlike passage through time, where music becomes a surrealist canvas that bends perception.

Yet through all of this—the shifts, the losses, the cosmic scale—"Intangible Harmonies" reminds me that the music within remains untouched. It is a sanctuary beyond reach, immune to loss, living safely in the inner silence where no hand can grasp it.

# 12. METAMORPHOSIS NO. 9

**(Text set to music)**

*I hear shifting patterns over time*
*as my ephemeral creation*
*spins on an axis of creativity,*

*its form comes from a rich musical reservoir*
*of sparkling themes and motives;*

*as swift as rivers meandering through varied terrain,*
*my new auditory sensation*
*screams with joy*
*as you become a sounding board,*

*absorbing sonic vibrations*
*in a classical feast.*

*designed to lift your tattered spirits,*
*reborn with a fresh vitality for life,*

*you float to a new dimension*
*leaving behind your shell of burden*
*for a garden of possibilities and promises.*

# 13. MOON DUST
## (Text set to music)

*Moon dust settles in flakes of silver ions.*
*The millennium showers you with memories.*
*You walk in the shadows of people you never met.*
*They touch you in ways that affect your every movement.*
*The ions pass through your body, and you are blessed.*

## 14. CRAFTED STARDUST
**(Text set to music)**

*We are all crafted stardust,*
*floating on an island paradise,*

*sharing a common dream*
*revealed in conversation a day at a time;*

*reality is sculptured slowly,*
*with a chisel,*

*until a universal form*
*becomes self-evident,*

*our individual realities*
*are golden bits of stardust*

*strewn in fields of yellow streams*
*upon a stage*

*where we perform*
*to an audience*
*clapping at each curtain close.*

# 15. MILLENNIUM LOOPS
## (Revised text, original text set to music)

*Millennium loops—*

*hums and buzzes,*
*waterfalls bending into birdcalls,*
*glass shattering into lark song.*

*A play of sound,*
*a journey through space,*

*Dalí's clock melting*
*into persistence*

## 16. INTANGIBLE HARMONIES

### (Revised text, original text set to music)

*They can take my clothes,*
*my rings,*
*my books,*
*my house.*

*But not the music within me.*

*That harmony,*
*intangible,*
*beyond reach,*
*lives safe—*
*untouchable.*

## *Nature & Awe*

Artists follow their own beat, much like rivers carving their own destiny. Nature offers a rhythm older than human time, guiding us toward balance, resilience, and awe.

In "She Saw the Rainbow," the storm clears, and a rainbow arches across the mountains. It becomes a metaphor for renewal—the moment when grief yields to light, when nature itself sings of peace.

"The Japanese Gardens" honors another kind of beauty: the cultivated harmony passed through generations. Here, blossoms and ancestors mingle, embodying the delicate continuity between life, memory, and the living earth.

But not all encounters with nature are serene. In "When Dreaming Is Done," the dream world recedes, leaving only the ordinary day. It is a poem of unease, where the wondrous dissolves into routine and the dreamer feels the loss of transcendence.

## 17. SHE SAW THE RAINBOW
### (Revised text, original text set to music)

*After the storm,*
*she saw the rainbow*
*arched over the San Gabriels.*

*Thunder echoed miles away.*

*She stood, transfixed,*
*mindful of nature's call.*

*The sun rose to greet her,*
*and she sparkled with joy,*
*having heard the glorious*
*vibrations of a friend.*

# 18. THE JAPANESE GARDENS
**(Text set to music)**

*Florid delicate balances in constancy,*
*cultivating flowers for the bouquet.*
*Pink blossoms mature in a rich legacy.*

*Ancestors who choose to smell the rose that blooms,*
*upon a blue velvet pond glimmering in the night,*
*cast their shadows on the banks of the Japanese gardens.*

## 19. WHEN DREAMING IS DONE

**(Text set to music)**

*Upside-down in a universe that is right side up.*
*Sitting on Andy's lap as Edward Gorey draws us.*

*A glorious world of temporary thoughts erased,*
*as life turns into routines*
*that escaped all on board this spacecraft with no pilot.*

*Sounds are heard as being quite silent;*
*its meaning eclipsed by the rising sun*
*which begins the day when dreaming is done.*

## Grief & Connection

*When the artist dies,*
*we are left with a body of work*
*profound in its stature*
*and abundant in its totality.*
*– 1.11.2016*

Grief gives way to memory, and memory gives way to presence. Through loss, art continues to speak, carrying the voice of the absent into the present.

In "For the Dearly Departed," music becomes a bridge across mortality, flowing into the formless presence of those who are gone. Each note is both farewell and reunion, a whispered assurance that sound itself endures beyond death.

"One Note at a Time" offers meditation on patience and presence—how life, love, and creation are woven not in grand gestures but in small increments, steady as breath, until wholeness appears.

With "Little Gems," I turn toward the overlooked treasures of living. These scattered sparks, half-hidden in the bramble of routine, glow with quiet radiance when we pause long enough to notice.

And in "Music," the musicality of the language is appreciated: that universal force which transcends every boundary, reaching the psyche where no words can follow, bathing us in joy, transformation, and wonder.

## 20. FOR THE DEARLY DEPARTED

*You wait in silence*
*to hear crafted creations*
*from the appointed one,*
*guiding me*
*as I sit sculpturing with wonder and delight,*
*often thinking that you will get no chance*
*to hear this new opus.*

*But music has energy that never dies,*
*flowing beyond my senses*
*to your formless,*
*noble presence,*
*thereby giving reassuring nods*
*to divinely elegant*
*black and white notations.*

## 21. ONE NOTE AT A TIME

**(Text set to music)**

*One note at a time will bring you to completeness,*

*one thought at a time is all it takes,*
*one word builds on another,*
*one flame to keep your eyes focused,*
*one world is what we have.*

*a large living organism,*
*which requires care and nourishment.*

*one lover to share your dreams,*
*one room where you can find solitude,*
*one vision to cling a hope to,*
*one star to wish upon,*

*One dream to cast your constructs to the wind.*

# 22. LITTLE GEMS

## (Text set to music)

*little gems*
*sparkle,*

*awaiting to be discovered,*

*as they shine*
*among the bramble*
*and the brier*
*of our busy lives;*

*we often don't see the glow of a jewel*
*as it merrily lingers,*

*and when discovery occurs,*

*we are surprised*
*and often startled,*
*as the gleam beckons you*
*to feel its eternal power and glory.*

## 23. MUSIC

*Music satisfies as no other medium can,*
*its power reaches deep into your psyche*
*giving you joy and elation*
*that cannot be matched anywhere by any other means;*

*This universal language speaks*
*to all who will listen,*
*for a moment*
*or for hours*
*to its rich sonority.*

*Riding air currents*
*in a flowing independence,*
*heralding the composer's thought*
*in a delicious soup*
*of sonic intensity,*

*You drink passionately*
*as it bathes you*
*with all its diverse wonder.*

## Struggle & Irony

*The lofty height of original music sits patiently awaiting premieres.*
*–3.19.2016*

Not all art is reverence and awe. Sometimes the creative life turns bitterly comic, caught between the purity of inspiration and the indifference of the world.

"My Compositions as Garbage Liners" is a satire born of frustration, a darkly humorous vision of scores discarded like trash when musicians demand payment to touch them. It is a biting commentary on the economics of art, the neglect of new music, and the absurdity of a system that prizes profit above creation.

By contrast, "My Music to Conquer" revels in performance's triumph: the thrill of thunderous cascades, the joy of sharing new sonic wonders with listeners hungry for release from the familiar. Here music becomes a celebration—a reminder of why we persist, why we climb onto the stage of life again and again.

Finally, "The Arts" expands the critique into a larger lament for culture itself. Painters unseen, composers unheard, writers unread, choreographers unwatched—the paradox of creative labor in a world hardened by commerce. And yet the poem closes with conviction: the artist creates because he must, because without the arts the soul itself goes silent. This final aphorism is both warning and credo, one of the clearest statements of my own belief in the essential role of art in human life.

# 24. MY COMPOSITIONS AS GARBAGE LINERS

**(Text set to music)**

*When bombs start dropping down on America*
*and there is no paper to buy,*
*folks will use my compositions as garbage liners.*

*It will be more practical*
*than getting musicians to play the damn scores!*

*You can't even get a musician to play a piano work,*
*yes it's true,*

*without a 500-dollar bill in hand!*

*So I suppose the black and white liners*
*will make an artistic statement*

*to someone*
*who is tone deaf*

*at the Visual Art Museum for Modern Composers.*

# 25. MY MUSIC TO CONQUER

*The performer delighted in the notion of music to conquer;*

*To display his talents on a stage with a nine-foot Steinway at his fingertips*
*dressed with black tie and polished shoes;*
*He rolled thunderous cascades of sound into a hall of curious onlookers,*
*craving a menu of new sonic wonders*
*to add to their harmonic encyclopedic repertory*
*of musical tastes and inventions;*

*Knowing that what people really need*
*is a break from the familiar patterns*
*that make up our existence.*

## 26. THE ARTS (REVISED TEXT)

### (Originally titled "The Arts in America," 7/8/2001)

*The painter draws a world unfamiliar to those who cannot see,*
*The composer crafts a musical gem for those who do not listen,*
*The writer invents a cast of characters for a novel not read,*
*The choreographer sketches a dance for the stage that no one watches.*

*Who will nourish the fragile seed of art,*
*in a soil hardened by commerce and neglect?*

*What hand will shield the gifted few,*
*left untended in the shadow of greed?*

*Where is the voice that rises to defend*
*the value of beauty in a barren age?*

*Attuned to the human condition,*
*the artist creates to satisfy an inner need,*

*Completing each work*
*with the confidence of a true craftsman,*

*Expressing a desire to build*
*on his aesthetic foundations,*

*A world unique, defining a sensibility for those*
*choosing to see, listen, read or watch—*

*for without the arts, the soul goes silent.*

## Closing Reflections

Through these poems, the themes of mystery, transformation, and unpredictability emerge with clarity. Creativity is not something I own—it owns me. It channels itself through dream, memory, silence, and longing. I have come to see that poetry and music are not separate languages but dialects of the same soul. Each composition, each poem, has helped me cross invisible thresholds—from sorrow to wonder, from confusion to clarity—giving voice to what might otherwise remain buried.

For the unknown composer—for me—these poems are a record of presence: a way to be seen and heard without shouting. A reminder that even in a world distracted by noise, the quiet pulse of an honest voice still matters.

# CODA

## A Gallery of Favorites

Over the years, certain poems have revealed themselves as touchstones of my artistic identity. They carry within them a resonance that continues to echo through my life as both poet and composer.

### CONDUITS (2003)

***(Full poem in Chapter 13)***

*On becoming a vessel for sound beyond oneself:*

This poem feels like a keystone in my creative life. It captures my belief that I am not the source of music, but the vessel through which it flows. I believe that it has strength, humility, and purpose—something I've returned to many times while composing. Its imagery of being a channel for music resonates with my lifelong view of creativity as mystical, spontaneous, and larger than self.

### HOW DO I BEGIN? (8/22/2025)

*On the struggle of beginnings and the inevitability of creation:*

*When revelations*
*are obscured by*
*density of thoughts,*
*the seamless*
*are as plentiful*
*as broken transitions.*

*I strain to bring forth*
*meanings from*
*meditative ramblings*
*and obscure figurative*
*lack of interpretations.*

*Senseless and becoming*
*are brain fuel,*
*metaphorically speaking,*
*thus your experiences*
*are whole and inevitable*
*when rational continuities*
*are plentiful.*

Here, the density and uncertainty of thought wrestle with the necessity of expression. It is a reminder that creation is never smooth; it begins in obscurity, yet from that obscurity something inevitable and whole emerges.

## LET MUSIC (1/19/2024)

*This poem is my credo in miniature, written as a flowing litany of music's powers:*

*Let music*
*heal your soul,*
*keep you focused,*
*transport you,*
*give you peace,*
*stir passion within,*
*calm you,*
*excite your senses,*
*be a beacon of inspiration,*
*keep you in the present,*

*reinvigorate reasons to be alive,*
*elevate your mood,*
*send you to worlds unknown,*
*and*
*focus your attention on the now.*

I love this poem for its pure affirmation of music's healing and transformative powers. It distills my philosophy: music focuses us on the present, transports us, and reinvigorates our reasons for being alive. This personal artistic statement, dressed in lyric form, reads like a prayer to the art that sustains me.

## SHE SAW THE RAINBOW (2003/2012)

***(Full poem in Chapter 13)***

This one is luminous and tender. It reflects my belief in humanity's deep connection with nature: we are part of it, not separate from it. And while carrying a note of gratitude—for beauty, for healing, for survival after difficulty—there's something timeless about the image of witnessing a rainbow. It is both intimate and universal at once.

## ADVICE ON MUSICAL DRAFTS (1/26/24)

***(Full poem in Chapter 13)***

*On embracing spontaneity and the refining hand of editing:*

This poem is playful and wise at the same time. It reflects my trust in the editing process, my openness to spontaneity, and my refusal to overcontrol the flow of creation. It balances humor with seriousness, turning what could be "dry craft advice" into a living philosophy of surprise and joy.

## THE MUSIC BECOMES ITS OWN REWARD (8/21/2024)

***(Full poem in Chapter 14)***

*On embracing spontaneity and the refining hand of editing:*

This one is a summation—quiet, clear, and profound. It reads almost like a farewell, but instead of sadness, it leaves us with a gift: the reminder that the act of creating itself is enough. It doesn't rely on audience, fame, or permanence. It's my philosophy of art, condensed into a final, resonant chord.

These poems serve as a gallery of touchstones, echoing the arc of my artistic life. They affirm that art does not ask for permission to exist—it simply insists on being. And in that insistence lies both struggle and reward, irony and reverence, grief and joy.

# PART IV

## You Are Your Musical Constructs

# CHAPTER 13

## My Musical Aesthetics

*"One's ear needs to be developed just like a composer's musical flowering, which is continually growing and taking a new shape."*
– JAC

*"Aesthetic sensibility demands intelligent use of musical material."*
– JAC

*"There is a fearlessness about Carollo's writing that can only come from speaking from the heart."*
*– FANFARE*

I have alluded to my aesthetics throughout this book—woven between memories, moments of inspiration, and the unfolding story of a life in music. In this chapter, I turn directly to the task of articulation. Here, I gather short essays, notes, and reflections written over many years—some formal, others spontaneous—as a way of drawing a clearer portrait of my evolving musical aesthetics.

These writings serve as fragments of understanding—glimpses into the principles, impulses, and philosophies that have guided my creative process. Through them, I attempt to define, as best I can, what music means to me: how it originates, how it grows, how it speaks.

Together, these essays reveal recurring themes: the importance of spontaneity, the role of intuition, the dialogue between structure and surprise, the metaphysical roots of sound, and the necessity of remaining in the moment—insights gathered from a lifetime of listening, creating, and becoming.

## On Spontaneity and the Unfolding Form

*Spontaneity lets the artist act freely in the moment.*
*Be unconcerned with the product's fate.*

Trusting in the unknown is the single thread that runs through the fabric of my compositional life. One should never feel compelled to impose rigid structures onto the music at the outset. To do so would be to deny the music its freedom to breathe, to become what it must become. Instead, I begin with a gesture—a motif, a phrase, a fragment—and I listen. Not just with the ears, but with intuition. The music, when it arrives authentically, tells me where it wants to go.

Predefining the form too early closes off the pathways to discovery. Structure, when it emerges organically, supports the spirit of the piece rather than constraining it. This allows the music to unfold like a living thing—shaped not by expectation, but by necessity.

Spontaneity is not carelessness. It is discipline without rigidity. It is the openness to follow a musical idea wherever it leads, even into uncharted territory. It is a form of listening to the unconscious, to the ether, where all art begins. In this state, surprise becomes a tool, not an accident. And if I am surprised by what emerges, chances are the listener will be, too.

## Regarding Form

*Form should emerge from the content;*
*let your material guide your structure.*

There is a quiet danger in forcing music into a mold too soon—an impulse to "stuff" sound into the shell of a structure before it has spoken its truth. Though form can offer guidance, it must never dictate the soul of a piece. Music, like life, resists confinement when it is most alive.

To impose a preconceived form on a new composition is to silence its own internal compass. You may start with an idea—a motif, a texture, a gesture whispered by the ether—but its unfolding must be allowed to breathe. To strangle it within the corset of sonata form or the neat expectations of an A-B-A design too early is to rob it of surprise, evolution, and spontaneity. The risk is a music that feels constructed rather than born.

I have learned that form should be a response, not a command. As leaves emerge from a tree at springtime, so too should music emerge from its content. Music speaks when it is ready, and its architecture arises from the needs of the material. The best structures are discovered in hindsight, revealed by the contours of the journey, not charted in advance like a map imposed on unknown terrain.

True creativity invites risk, ambiguity, and the joy of discovery. It thrives in the moment when you say, "I don't know where this is going, but I trust it." Let the material shape its own destiny. Listen deeply. Follow its lead. Eventually, the piece will reveal its own architecture—one that is authentic, coherent, and intimately tied to its voice.

When form is born from within, rather than stuffed from without, the result is a living thing. A piece that breathes. A work that speaks. A music that becomes not just an artifact of craft, but a vessel of truth.

## *The Composer as Conduit*

*We are conduits, a vehicle to the other world of bliss and ecstasy.*

One of the most enduring convictions I hold is that the composer is not the sole originator of the music. Rather, we are conduits—receptors of something greater, more mysterious, something that flows through us rather than from us. I have long sensed that the true source of music lies in realms beyond conscious control, arriving from the ether, from the unconscious, from the vast interior world where thought dissolves and feeling takes form.

It is a highly personal language, and every astute composer has their stamp in the first measure, system, or ten seconds of tape—whatever the medium. We know it is Bach, for example, within the first several bars.

When composing, I often feel more like a listener than a creator. A vessel. The ideas that emerge are not summoned—they arrive. My responsibility is to shape them, respect them, not distort them through over-analysis or ego. This humility before the act of creation is vital. It demands silence, solitude, and a willingness to be surprised.

I've spoken of the dream state—that in-between world where imagination is free of constraints. This is where I find the music. The editing comes later, but the initial impulse must remain untamed, intuitive, and pure.

To be a conduit is not to be passive. It is to be open. Open to mystery, open to feeling, open to the strange and beautiful forces that call themselves music. In this way, *composition becomes both a spiritual and artistic act—a conversation between the seen and unseen, the known and the ineffable.*

## Let the Listener Be Surprised

*Keep the listener suspended in discovery.*

Predictability is the enemy of engagement. If I already know exactly what comes next, the music risks becoming stale—formulaic. But if I don't know what's coming, then I remain alert, alive in the moment. This sense of surprise becomes a kind of magic, shared between composer and listener.

Music is not just structure—it is tension, release, mystery, and revelation. It must move forward with purpose, but without a map. This does not mean abandoning form but allowing form to emerge through discovery. Freshness must be built into the DNA of the piece.

There is deep pleasure in the unexpected—a sudden shift in texture, a haunting chord, a silence that lingers. These are not tricks; they are invitations. Invitations to the listener to lean in, to follow, to wonder. When surprise is earned, it becomes emotional. It deepens the experience.

And so, I compose in such a way that even I am surprised. I listen back and ask, "Where did that come from?" It's a good question—one that leads not to answers, but to awe.

## Music in the Present Tense

*Everything must be new.*

Music exists only now. Each note arrives and vanishes, like breath. This impermanence is its power. Unlike a painting or a book, music must be experienced in time, moment by moment. It teaches us to listen not just with our ears, but with our attention.

When I compose, I aim to *sustain this presence*—to create music that demands to be heard as it unfolds. You are there, or you are not. And if you are there, fully, you enter into communion with the sound, with the silence, with yourself.

This is why *momentum matters*. Each gesture must carry meaning. Each phrase must lead to the next with emotional necessity. When music loses its sense of immediacy, it becomes decoration. But when it lives in the present tense, it becomes a force—one that can move, disturb, uplift, awaken.

For me, *composing is a way to remain in the eternal present*. The music keeps me centered, focused, and fully aware. And in that awareness, I find peace.

## Editing Toward Essence

*Let form be flexible, responsive, and emergent.*

The first draft is rarely the final destination. It is a beginning—a block of marble, still unformed. Editing is not just correction; it is an act of listening more deeply to what the music wants to be.

Often, the initial impulse comes quickly. But clarity follows only through revision. I return to the material again and again, removing excess, clarifying textures, and adjusting pacing. I listen not just for what is there, but for what is essential.

There is great joy in this process—not unlike carving. With each pass, I chip away at what distracts. I heighten what moves. I may not know in advance what the final shape will be, but I trust that it will reveal itself.

Through this process, the music reveals its true nature. And in doing so, it becomes more capable of speaking directly to others.

## *From Silence, Everything*

*Without silence, music has no contrast.*

Before the first note, there is silence—not absence, but *a sacred stillness where possibility dwells.* I have often felt that silence is not a void but a presence. It listens. It waits. It invites.

The best ideas come when I am in moments of quiet contemplation. Composing begins with listening—to the self, yes, but also to something deeper, more ancient. Silence gives way to sound, and sound gives shape to emotion.

Even within the music, silence remains. A held breath. A pause. A space between notes. These are where meaning often lives.

I return again and again to this truth: *Music finds its origins not in sound, but in the focused contemplation of silence, which is full of potential.*

## The Music Is Always with Me

*I do not wait for inspiration. It is simply there—*
*always present, like breath.*

Music has never been separate from who I am. It lives in my bloodstream, embedded in thought, in silence.

Even when I am not writing, the music continues. I trust this inner current. I shape it. I let it speak. Some days it flows easily. Other times it resists. But it never abandons me.

This constant companionship brings both comfort and responsibility. I must listen. I must honor the gift. And I must give it form with integrity because the music asks to be made real.

The music is not an external goal. It is my interior landscape. It is my purpose, my quiet rebellion against forgetting.

To say "I am a composer" is an expression of being. The music is always with me. It always has been. It always will be.

## Composing at the Edge of Mystery

*The act of composing is my way of touching the ineffable.*

There is a place where knowledge dissolves—where technique fades into intuition. That is where I compose. Not in perfect clarity, but at the edge of mystery.

Every piece requires a leap. I must step off the edge. Let go of control. Trust that something larger is guiding the way.

To compose in this space requires courage. It means listening without expectation, following an invisible thread. It holds a mirror to the soul.

Yet it is precisely in this uncertainty that meaning resides. I do not write to explain. *I write to explore.* And if I have done my work well, the listener may hear it too—not as an answer, but as a shared encounter with the unknown.

## *On Emotion and the Present Moment, A Philosophical Treatise*

*Music's truest purpose is to awaken presence.*

Emotion can only arise—it cannot be summoned or defined in advance. It is an event—a living vibration in time. Emotion, like music, is inseparable from the moment in which it is born. Both are temporal experiences, existing only as they unfold. To name it too soon is to lose it.

Music, to me, is a condition where emotion can awaken. The sound itself, in its pure form, offers the listener a mirror in which to find their own reflection. Each hearing becomes a unique act of recognition, a dialogue between the inner and outer worlds.

Descriptors in music—words like *dolce, agitato,* or *misterioso*—serve as suggestions. They are mood invitations. The performer must inhabit the score and give it breath. Their understanding, shaped by their life and present state of being, becomes the music's true form. The composer sets the framework, knowing the performer will ignite its spirit. In this sense, the emotional truth of music is never fixed. It is continually reborn in the act of listening and performance.

No two interpretations can ever be identical because no two moments in time are ever the same. What was once interpreted as sorrow may later be construed as calm acceptance; what was once yearning may now feel like peace. To compose, then, is to trust—to release control, to let music exist in its own time, as an unfolding presence. In that unfolding, both composer and listener meet in a shared now—the sacred instant where sound becomes experience, and emotion becomes alive.

## *Closing Reflections*

*Music uniquely needs both creator and interpreter.*

I have long believed that music lives in the present tense. It is the art of *now*—a form that resists possession. To compose is to dwell within the moment of its becoming. The sounds that emerge are living gestures, evolving, breathing, and then vanishing into silence.

In this way, every composition becomes a meditation on impermanence—a reminder that emotion, like sound, must be *experienced*. The performer, in their sensitivity and imagination, renews the life of the score each time they play. And the listener, through their own heart, completes the circle of creation.

If my music succeeds in anything, it is in offering this fleeting encounter: a moment where emotion arises and meaning blooms without command. In that delicate exchange, music fulfills its truest purpose—to awaken presence and to remind us that beauty is in what *becomes*.

*Every piece deserves its own character, pace, and logic.*

My music exists on the edge of tonality—not fully tonal, nor strictly atonal—but dwelling in a realm best described as *pantonality*. Coined by R. Réti in 1958, pantonality describes music that contains all keys simultaneously—not the absence of a tonal center, but the presence of all centers at once.

This simultaneous inclusion of all tonalities gives the music an improvisational quality. The excitement in my *Orchestra Concerto: Longinus, On Sublimity (Great Thoughts, Noble Dictions, Strong Emotions)* (2019)—a work not yet published—arises from this very technique. Pantonality affirms that ambiguity is not confusion; rather, it is a deliberate artistic choice. It enables the creation of tension and release, of climax and anticlimax, of uncertainty in counterpoint with expectation. These contrasts become the living breath of the music, keeping the listener suspended in a state of ongoing discovery.

Through this approach, one may construct musical architectures that are not only fresh and unpredictable but deeply engaging—both emotionally and intellectually. In doing so, this ambiguous musical language becomes a worthy rival to the tonal tradition: equal in expressive power and capable of conjuring its own moments of glory, awe, and revelation.

Music is an art whose *perfection always lies in the next performance.* Studio recordings demand multiple takes; live moments embrace their flaws. Yet, by focusing on particular details, we find joy. Perhaps the goal is not perfection, but presence. To escape paralysis—and enjoy the moment.

*Composition parallels psychology.* In clinical work, I once studied the principle of "tightening and loosening"—the expansion or contraction of perspective as therapy unfolds.

Music behaves in kind. We stretch or compress ideas while composing and revising. Musical phrases, like sentences, can shift meaning with each iteration.

### *Final Thoughts*

These essays are markers for a journey, waypoints along a path that continues to unfold. My musical aesthetics are living ideas, not fixed doctrines. What binds them is a spirit of openness: to silence, to surprise, to mystery, and to the music itself.

The one enduring truth I return to is this: *Music is something we enter,* not merely something we create. And once inside, we find ourselves changed.

Compose urgently. Extract from your imagination the raw materials for a new work. Capture the moment of clarity when intention crystallizes. The present is all we have.

*The music becomes its own reward.* And so, I continue—listening, shaping, trusting—composing from wonder, not from dogmatic certainty. Music is always a work in progress; we need to value *process over conclusion* and view mystery as a source of inspiration.

As I moved forward with my musical career, I took to heart what Bob once told me: *You don't need to compose any more music; the work you're proud of will be what defines you.*

And yet, I continued—despite his generous words—because I could never stop.

*I could never abandon the reason for my existence.* I could never stop loving Bill.

# CHAPTER 14

## Reflections, Legacy, and Letting Go

As I grow older, reflection comes more often—not just on what I've created, but on what remains undone, the choices that have shaped my journey, and a quiet understanding that not every note will be heard, nor every poem fully grasped. And that's okay.

I never composed for fame, applause, or accolades. I composed because I had no choice. Music was, and still is, how I make sense of the world—how I process memory, pain, joy, and the unknowable. My music, like my poetry, is survival. It is breath. It is blood. It is silence made articulate.

Looking back on my early life with my adoptive parents, I see now how deeply they shaped me. They lived with honor and healthy rituals—spiritual worship, shared moments, closeness to the Earth and respect for its generosity. Somehow, despite hardship, I absorbed these lessons without realizing it. It's like the old saying: You only learn to appreciate what you've lost once it's no longer there.

Why search for birth parents, when my adoptive ones had given me comfort, love, safety, and support? Why look if I believed both birth parents were gone? Why reopen that wound if abandonment was all I expected to find?

The life I had with Bill explains the delay. Sometimes I told myself that if Rosanna had truly abandoned me, she'd find a way to reach out—that she'd want to see her son after years of guilt. I was wrong, of course. But deep down, I knew I had to do it on my own terms.

I waited for Bill's passing, for grieving to settle, for my authentic self to flower before I began the search. I don't regret the timing. You can lose yourself in love—two spirits merging into one. When your stamina tells you it's time, you open the doors to opportunity, hope for the best, and step forward to unearth the mysteries of your beginning.

*Life unfolds as it happens, but it's often only defined after you're gone.*

To walk unknown through a city is a sacred act. It offers freedom to be authentic. Some never find that bliss. In composing, authenticity matters. I didn't find my voice until I stopped trying to emulate Bach—the immortal Baroque master.

Music historians analyze rhythmic, harmonic, and melodic patterns that form a composer's language. A music viewer once told me my music was "vertical." Scholars dissect compositions not only in the composer's lifetime but long after they're dead. It's a never-ending conversation for the greats—Mozart, Bach, Beethoven—their music endlessly examined.

There's an unspoken truth that some professors might find uncomfortable. Pianist Michael Sayers put it simply: "The greatest music can't be devised step-by-step. It's as if it comes from somewhere outside our minds, beyond time. Otherwise, anyone could study 18th-century harmony and counterpoint and become Mozart!"

*Creativity is internal—unexplained as it happens.*

Spontaneity is its root; the moment music flows onto the page or into thin air, so it can be enjoyed now and for generations to come. Marvel at its beauty. Savor its permanence.

Long after the creative act leaves you, joy overwhelms,

knowing its essence will never be destroyed or replaced.

Through mindfulness, openness, and spontaneity, I've tried to bring something deeply personal and universally resonant into the world. The interplay between tangible and intangible, the recognition of hidden beauty and meaning in everyday life, runs throughout my poetry and music. Art becomes a channel for discovery and a way to express deeper truths.

Looking back on my catalogue, I see a diary not in words but sound. Pieces like *Let Thy Mind Be Still* offer quiet reflection, while *Transcendence in the Age of War* confronts urgency and loss. Each carries fragments of my life—the joys, grief, and questions that linger. To those who listen, I offer not just music, but a story told in silence and sound, a conversation that continues long after the final note.

With many works behind me—poems, piano and guitar pieces, duets, trios, quartets, symphonies, and vocal works—I look back in awe. Not because I believe I created something eternal, but because it happened at all. I never expected a life so immersed in creative expression. Yet here we are.

Letting go is not giving up. It's gently releasing the need to control the outcome. I have done the work. I have given voice to the unknown child I once was. That boy from the Institute for Infants in Torino—Giovanni Baudino—now rests comfortably in the identity I built: composer and poet John A. Carollo.

I accept that many works will never be performed, many poems never read aloud. But they exist. They matter. They live on the page, the score, the ears of a few, and the soul of their maker.

In the end, that is enough.

I once wrote: *Music unheard is more valuable than music heard.* Perhaps that is the heart of it. The value lies not in public reception but in private necessity. Each piece was born from a truth—a mystery, a question needing voice. It's been my privilege to give them form.

If anyone reads this years from now, perhaps long after I'm gone, I hope they hear what I tried to say: beauty is always within reach, solitude is fertile ground, imagination is sacred, and music—even if unheard—is never lost.

I let go, knowing I held on long enough. All great music must end—the moment its death is inevitable, when we all die with it. But during its exhilarating existence, we celebrate the highs and lows, the sensual conversation leading to climaxes, glorifying life's joy.

*The music becomes its own reward.*

# THE MUSIC BECOMES ITS OWN REWARD

*I will have to die*
*before anyone takes real notice.*

*Joining the living dead will be a comfort.*

*After all, it's the work of dead composers*
*who get attention these days.*

*No more dolling out cash*
*to musicians who need to feed their families.*
*No more dreaming that someday*
*a musician will ask for a score, learn it,*
*and perform it without pay—*
*the music becoming its own reward.*

*In the meantime,*
*I will remember*
*what my composition teacher told me years ago:*

*"John, your path will follow*
*the footsteps of those long gone.*
*You've composed enough music.*
*You will be remembered for*
*a handful of pieces."*

*A sentiment that doesn't pay the bills,*
*but one that captures*
*my heart and puts a smile*
*on my face.*

# EPILOGUE

## A Life in Sound and Silence

In the end, all I ever wanted was to listen—to the faint stirrings of inspiration, the whispers of dreams, the truths buried beneath silence. Music and poetry were never careers for me. They were callings, compulsions, sacred devotions. They gave me a voice when I had none, purpose when I wandered, and meaning when the world felt senseless.

From the earliest days, when sound was mystery and silence, a canvas, I felt pulled toward something beyond words. It was never about fame or recognition. It was about connection—to me, to others, to something greater than the sum of our parts. Every note composed, every line written was a thread woven into the fabric of my existence.

To have lived as a composer and poet has been my great joy and labor. Whether my works reach many ears or only a few, they remain the truest expression of who I am. They are my legacy, my offering, my conversation with eternity. In the quiet moments when no one listens—that's when music and poetry mean the most—they are the language of my soul speaking freely.

There were times when doubt crept in, and the world's indifference weighed heavily. Yet even then, the need to create never faded. It was a flame that could not be extinguished—a stubborn fire that fueled every hour spent alone with my thoughts, my instruments, my pen. Creation was both refuge and rebellion, a way to claim space in a world that often felt overwhelming.

To anyone encountering this book, I offer my deepest gratitude. You are a witness to a life shaped by the mysteries of sound and the revelations of verse. I hope you find here not only the story of one unknown composer but echoes of your own longing, resilience, and wonder.

This book is more than a collection of thoughts and musical titles; it is a map of my inner landscape, a record of the unseen struggles and triumphs that shaped me. It is proof that even in solitude, we are never truly alone. Our stories ripple outward, touching lives in ways we may never fully understand.

Talking about my music never interested me—my music spoke for itself. It carries the weight of joy and sorrow, moments of clarity and confusion, the mundane and the miraculous. To listen is to hear the musical diary of my life—a journey marked by both silence and sound.

As I close this chapter of my story, I do so with peace. The music lives on, beyond me, beyond time. It is a whisper in the wind, a pulse in the quiet, a reminder that we all leave traces—small or vast—on the world we pass through.

May you, too, find your voice in the silence, your song in the stillness, and your truth in the spaces between.

# AUTHOR'S NOTE

This collection is the culmination of a lifetime spent listening, creating, and seeking meaning beyond the obvious. The poems and music within these pages are fragments of a journey—a conversation between silence and sound, between the known and the mysterious.

I have never sought recognition or acclaim. My work is born of necessity, from a deep need to express what words alone cannot contain. I hope these pieces resonate with anyone who's ever felt creativity as both refuge and rebellion.

To the readers, listeners, and fellow travelers who find their way here—thank you for bearing witness. Your presence gives these works life beyond my own experience and breathes new meaning into the stories I have shared.

May you find in this collection the courage to embrace your own voice—however quiet or bold—and the comfort of knowing that in creating, we are never truly alone.

With gratitude,
**John A. Carollo**

# ACKNOWLEDGMENTS

I extend my deepest gratitude to the spirits—both seen and unseen (to AI who served as an editing assistant)—who have guided and sustained me throughout this journey.

To Bill Dresser, my beloved, whose unwavering love sustained me and whose memory continues to resonate within my music.

To David Greger, my cherished companion in Portland, a devoted connoisseur of the arts and the most brilliant historian I have ever known. Your passion and presence enrich my life immeasurably. Thank you, David, for your steadfast support. I hope our shared journey finds its way into a future continuation.

To my friends and fellow artists who believed in my music when recognition was scarce, and who so generously lent their talents to bring my compositions to life—I am profoundly grateful.

To Bob Lord and PARMA Recordings, your collaboration has opened invaluable doors and amplified my voice with great honor.

To every performer, engineer, and listener who has taken the time to engage with my compositions, your attention has rendered the silence meaningful.

To the librarians, curators, and archivists entrusted with preserving our cultural heritage—including the dedicated staff at Hamilton Library at the University of Hawai'i at Manoa—your vigilance ensures that stories such as mine endure, and that the legacy of Edward Gorey is forever honored.

Finally, to the reader, I offer my sincere thanks for attending to the music behind these words. May you carry a fragment of this work with you, inspiring your own creative endeavors.

# APPENDIX A

## Selected Works and Titles Referenced in the Memoir

### *Part Titles*

- **Part I – Origins**

Exploring the roots of identity, early influences, and the formative experiences that shaped the composer's worldview and creative voice.

- **Part II – Awakenings**

A period of discovery and self-realization, marked by the emergence of authentic expression and deeper artistic purpose.

- **Part III – Busy Being Born**

The ongoing process of transformation and growth, embracing change and the complexities of life through music and poetry.

- **Part IV – You Are Your Musical Constructs**

Reflections on the intertwining of self and creative output, and how identity is shaped by the art one creates.

## *Key Compositions Referenced*

- **Opus 1: Piano Suite No. 1 for Solo Piano (The Crumb Suite) (1997)**

The composer's first work, blending traditional piano techniques with personal motifs inspired by visual art.

- **Piano Suite No. 4 for Three Pianos (2005)**

A complex and layered piece using the unique textures possible with three pianos to explore interplay and dialogue. These textures later informed larger orchestral works.

- **Anguish in Every Household for Orchestra (2008–2010)**

An orchestral expression of universal themes—pain, endurance, and the quiet resilience found in daily life.

- **Themes for Edward Gorey for Solo Piano (1996)**

An homage to the whimsical and darkly imaginative illustrator Edward Gorey.

- **Metamorphosis I–III (for Solo Viola, Solo Violin) (2001)**

Music exploring the nature of transformation, both internal and external.

- **Symphony No. 5 – Classic Beauty Over Surface Novelty (Terminal Originality) (2022–2023)**

A symphonic reflection on the tension between tradition and innovation in modern composition.

- **Romantica Passione Suite for Guitar and Violin (2004)**

A passionate duet evoking a romantic narrative through lyrical interplay.

- **Trio for Piano, Guitar, and Violin (2002)**

An exuberant chamber work interweaving distinct instrumental voices in exciting and challenging dynamic conversations.

- **Guitar Suite No. 1 – Saggese Guitar Suite (Homage to Paganini) (2006–2007)**

A virtuosic suite for classical guitar honoring the legendary violinist Paganini.

- **Awakenings for String Orchestra (2013)**

A luminous piece symbolizing renewal and inner awakening.

- **Piano Suite No. 3 for Solo Piano (2002)**

A frenetic and emotionally charged suite of pianistic expression.

- **The Rhetoric and Mythos of Belief for String Orchestra (2014)**

A philosophical suite investigating faith, ideology, and the search for meaning through musical narrative—in memory of Bill.

- **Let Thy Mind Be Still for String Orchestra (2009)**

A calming, meditative work inviting listeners into quiet reflection and inner peace.

- **Transcendence in the Age of War for Concert Band (In Memory of 9/11) (2004–2009)**

A tribute to those affected by tragedy, memorializing resilience and sorrow.

- **Starry Night for String Orchestra (2009)**

A dark, vital, inventively written composition inspired by Van Gogh's *Starry Night Over the Rhône* (1888), *Musée d'Orsay, Paris.*

- **Quartet No. 1 for Clarinet in B-flat, Violin, Cello, and Piano (A Worded Grey Enigma) (2000)**

A chamber piece for Edward Gorey, exploring enigmatic and introspective themes through contrasting instrumental textures.

- **Busy Being Born for String Orchestra (2022)**

A celebration of growth, change, and the continual unfolding of life.

- **Burlesque for Trumpet in B-flat and Classical Guitar (2007)**

A playful, spirited duet embracing humor and theatrical flair.

- **Piano Etude No. II "Sightless" (2005)**

A technically demanding etude exploring virtuosity and inner vision.

- **Phantasmamusica for Solo Piano – Books I–VI (2019–2025)**

A multi-volume series of evocatively fantastic and complex piano works.

- **Symphony No. 3 (2017)**

A symphonic meditation on the transformative quietude of nature.

- **The Transfiguration of Giovanni Baudino for Piano and Orchestra (2008–2010)**

A deeply personal work tracing the composer's transformation—from mysterious origins to artistic clarity.

- **Awake Humanity to Nature's Beauty (Violin Version) (2011)**

A lyrical appeal to recognize and cherish the splendor of the natural world.

- **The Path Is Ambiguous for Solo Piano**

From a set of *Piano Preludes, Book II* (2001), a whimsical piece that entertains and satisfies.

- **Piano Etude No. 14 (Passing on Ancient Skills) (2001)**

A meditation on lineage and transmission—history breathing in gesture.

*[Note: The full score is provided separately at the end of the memoir.]*

## *Albums Mentioned*

- **Ampersand (2006)**

A collection of early chamber music, solo violin, and solo piano—revealing the composer's emerging voice.

- **Transcendence in the Age of War (2009)**

Featuring the *Saggese Guitar Suite*, a complex dedication to Paganini.

- **Starry Night (2011)**

An album of chamber and orchestral works containing core themes of darkness, beauty, and tension.

- **Volere (2012)**

A diverse selection of piano music, duets, and trios reflecting emotional range and stylistic curiosity.

- **Abrazo (2016)**

A jazz-influenced collaboration that also includes the composer's classical duet for trumpet and acoustic guitar.

- **The Transfiguration of Giovanni Baudino (2017)**

A landmark orchestral album featuring the piano and orchestral title piece that raises the composer's origin story out of obscurity.

- **Music From the Ethereal Side of Paradise (2018)**

A compilation of musical wonders featuring mature guitar pieces, bookended by string orchestra works typical of the composer's signature structure.

- **Sustain (2019)**

A collaborative album featuring solo piano works, continuing the evolution of expressive nuance and emotional depth through intimate performances.

- **Symphony No. 3 (2019)**

Based on the composer's settings of William Blake, this symphony celebrates nature and human love. It is full of invigorating lyrical drama, contained within a beautifully evocative world.

### *Texts Set to Music*

- **Poems by the Author (e.g., *"Little Gems," "Crafted Stardust"*)**

Personal poetry, which was often used as a lyrical foundation for vocal works.

- **William Blake**

The visionary Romantic poet whose works have inspired several musical settings.

- **Charles Bukowski**

The contemporary poet known for raw, confessional verse—infusing settings with grit and honesty.

- **Johann Wolfgang von Goethe**

A classic literary figure whose lyricism and philosophical scope offered rich material for musical adaptation.

- **Andrea Hollander**

A modern poet whose evocative imagery and emotional resonance align closely with the composer's sensibilities.

# APPENDIX B

The following artifacts relate to my 1959 transatlantic adoption from Italy to the United States, as documented in Chapter 1.

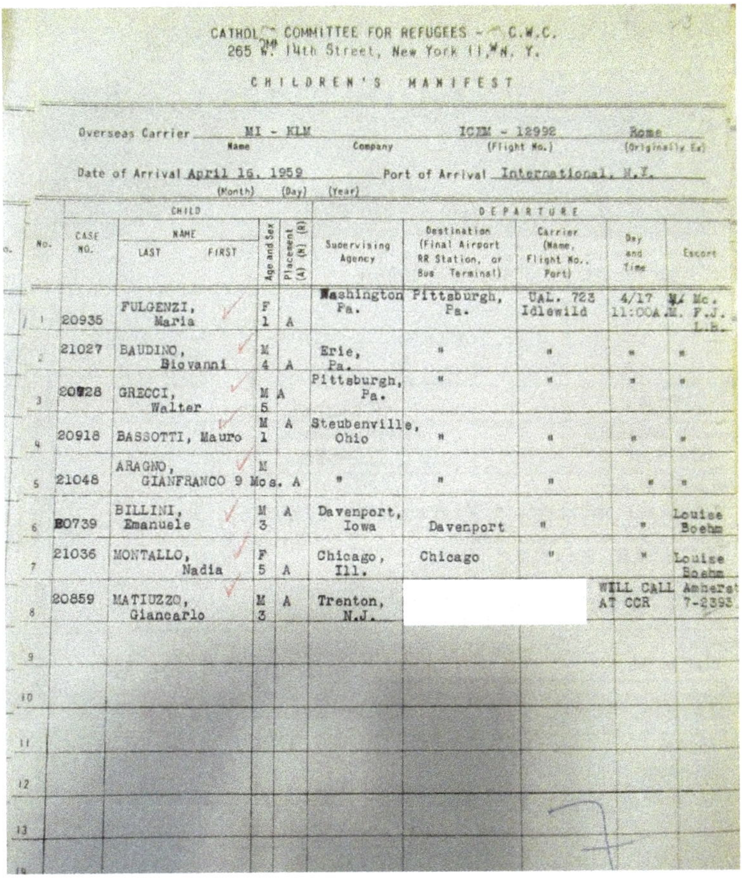

CATHOLIC COMMITTEE FOR REFUGEES - C.W.C.
265 W. 14th Street, New York 11, N. Y.

CHILDREN'S MANIFEST

Overseas Carrier MI - KLM (Name) (Company) ICEM - 12992 (Flight No.) Rome (Originally Ex)

Date of Arrival April 16, 1959 (Month) (Day) (Year) Port of Arrival International, N.Y.

| No. | CHILD: Case No. | CHILD: Name (Last, First) | Age and Sex | Placement (A) (N) (R) | DEPARTURE: Supervising Agency | Destination (Final Airport RR Station, or Bus Terminal) | Carrier (Name, Flight No., Port) | Day and Time | Escort |
|---|---|---|---|---|---|---|---|---|---|
| 1 | 20935 | FULGENZI, Maria | F 1 | A | Washington Pa. | Pittsburgh, Pa. | UAL. 723 Idlewild | 4/17 11:00A. | M. Mc. M. F.J. L.B. |
| 2 | 21027 | BAUDINO, Giovanni | M 4 | A | Erie, Pa. | " | " | " | " |
| 3 | 20[illegible]28 | GRECCI, Walter | M 5 | A | Pittsburgh, Pa. | " | " | " | " |
| 4 | 20918 | BASSOTTI, Mauro | M 1 | A | Steubenville, Ohio | " | " | " | " |
| 5 | 21048 | ARAGNO, GIANFRANCO | M 9 Mos. | A | " | " | " | " | " |
| 6 | B0739 | BILLINI, Emanuele | M 3 | A | Davenport, Iowa | Davenport | " | " | Louise Boehm |
| 7 | 21036 | MONTALLO, Nadia | F 5 | A | Chicago, Ill. | Chicago | " | " | Louise Boehm |
| 8 | 20859 | MATIUZZO, Giancarlo | M 3 | A | Trenton, N.J. | | | WILL CALL AT CCR | Amherst 7-2393 |
| 9 | | | | | | | | | |
| 10 | | | | | | | | | |
| 11 | | | | | | | | | |
| 12 | | | | | | | | | |
| 13 | | | | | | | | | |
| 14 | | | | | | | | | |

*Children's Manifest for Flight ICEM-12992*

*"The Flying Dutchman" of Royal Dutch Airlines*

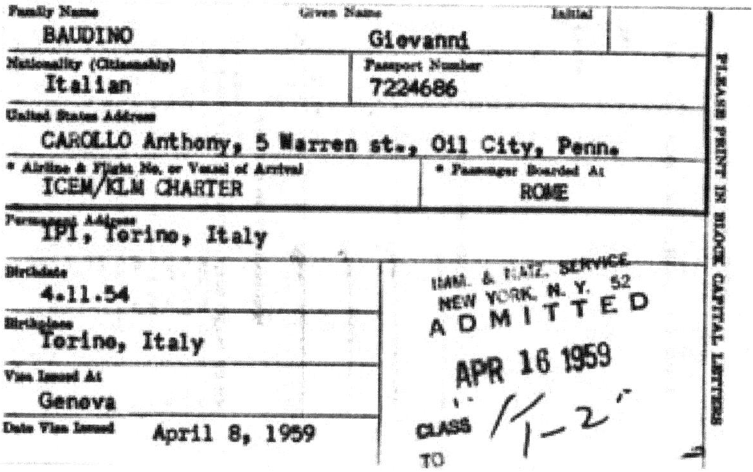

Family Name: BAUDINO
Given Name: Giovanni
Initial:
Nationality (Citizenship): Italian
Passport Number: 7224686
United States Address: CAROLLO Anthony, 5 Warren st., Oil City, Penn.
* Airline & Flight No. or Vessel of Arrival: ICEM/KLM CHARTER
* Passenger Boarded At: ROME
Permanent Address: IPI, Torino, Italy
Birthdate: 4.11.54
Birthplace: Torino, Italy
Visa Issued At: Genova
Date Visa Issued: April 8, 1959

IMM. & NATZ. SERVICE
NEW YORK, N. Y. 52
ADMITTED
APR 16 1959
CLASS
TO

PLEASE PRINT IN BLOCK CAPITAL LETTERS

*Typed Index Card with my adoptive parents' contact information.*

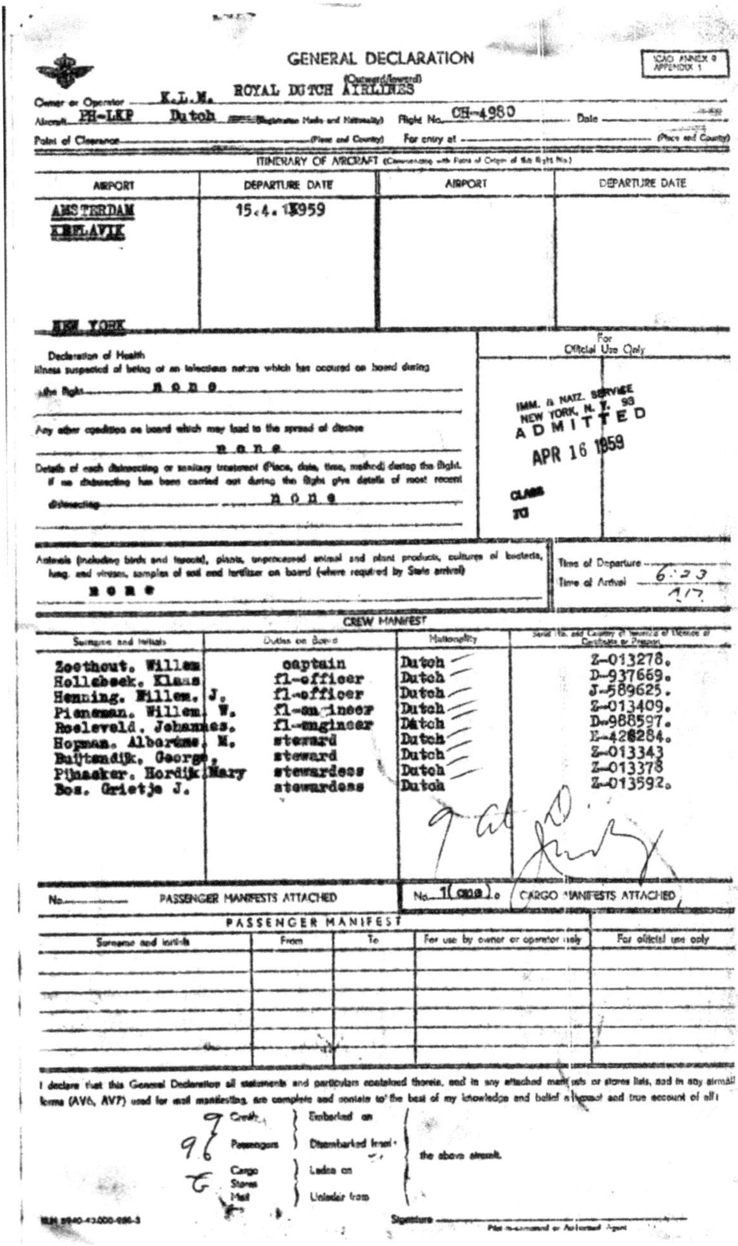

GENERAL DECLARATION (Outward/Inward)

ICAO ANNEX 9 APPENDIX 1

Owner or Operator K.L.M. ROYAL DUTCH AIRLINES

Aircraft PH-LKP Dutch (Registration Marks and Nationality) Flight No. CH-4980 Date

Point of Clearance (Place and Country) For entry at (Place and Country)

ITINERARY OF AIRCRAFT

| AIRPORT | DEPARTURE DATE | AIRPORT | DEPARTURE DATE |
| --- | --- | --- | --- |
| AMSTERDAM<br>KEFLAVIK<br>NEW YORK | 15.4.1959 | | |

Declaration of Health

Illness suspected of being of an infectious nature which has occurred on board during the flight none

Any other condition on board which may lead to the spread of disease none

Details of each disinsecting or sanitary treatment (Place, date, time, method) during the flight. If no disinsecting has been carried out during the flight give details of most recent disinsecting none

For Official Use Only

IMM. & NATZ. SERVICE NEW YORK, N. Y. 93 ADMITTED APR 16 1959 CLASS TO

Animals (including birds and insects), plants, unprocessed animal and plant products, cultures of bacteria, fung. and viruses, samples of soil and fertilizer on board (where required by State arrival) none

Time of Departure 6:23

Time of Arrival 4:17

CREW MANIFEST

| Surname and Initials | Duties on Board | Nationality | Serial No. and Country of Issuance of Licence or Certificate or Passport |
| --- | --- | --- | --- |
| Zoethout, Willem | captain | Dutch | Z-013278. |
| Hollebeek, Klaas | fl-officer | Dutch | D-937669. |
| Henning, Willem, J. | fl-officer | Dutch | J-589625. |
| Pieneman, Willem W. | fl-engineer | Dutch | Z-013409. |
| Roeleveld, Johannes. | fl-engineer | Dutch | D-988597. |
| Hopman, Alberdina M. | steward | Dutch | E-428284. |
| Buijtendijk, George. | steward | Dutch | Z-013343 |
| Pijnacker, Hordijk Mary | stewardess | Dutch | Z-013378 |
| Bos, Grietje J. | stewardess | Dutch | Z-013592. |

No. PASSENGER MANIFESTS ATTACHED No. 1 (one). CARGO MANIFESTS ATTACHED

PASSENGER MANIFEST

| Surname and initials | From | To | For use by owner or operator only | For official use only |
| --- | --- | --- | --- | --- |
| | | | | |

I declare that this General Declaration all statements and particulars contained therein, and in any attached manifests or stores lists, and in any airmail forms (AV6, AV7) used for mail manifesting, are complete and contain to the best of my knowledge and belief a full and true account of all

9 Crew, 96 Passengers, Cargo, Stores, Mail — Embarked on / Disembarked from / Laden on / Unladen from — the above aircraft.

Signature

Pilot in-command or Authorized Agent

*Declaration Form identifying the crew members and the captain, who was the legal guardian for the children on board during the flight.*

# APPENDIX C

## Selected Performances, Premieres & Recognitions

*The following represents a selection of premieres, collaborations, and creative projects that extended the reach of my compositions into concert halls, radio broadcasts, and visual media.*

### Premieres

- **Duet for Cello and Piano** – *We Will Never Witness Another of His Kind*

Ovidiu Marinescu, cello, and Noreen Cassidy-Polera, piano; *Carnegie Hall*, New York – September 28, 2024

- **Trio for Flute, Cello, and Piano – *Robust Constructs***

Trio Xia; *Orvis Auditorium*, Honolulu, HI – October 1, 2005

- **Piano Trio No. 1 for Piano, Violin, and Cello**

Trio Casals; *Philips Autograph Library*, West Chester University of Pennsylvania – May 9, 2015. This was followed by a *Carnegie Hall* performance on May 12, 2015.

- **Trio for Piano, Guitar, and Violin – 3rd Movement**

Duo 46 (Beth Ilana Schneider-Gould, violin; Matt Gould, guitar) and Nathanael May, piano; *Monti del Parterre Amphitheater,* Cortona, Italy – July 21, 2006

- **Awake Humanity to Nature's Beauty** (Blake Song Cycle) (Violin Version)

Stark Duo, Sachi P. Hirakouji, and I-Bei Lin; Live broadcast premiere, *Hawai'i Public Radio*, Honolulu – August 25, 2012

- **Metamorphosis No. 1 for Solo Viola**

*Ljova Zhurbin; The rRed Elephant Café*, Honolulu – July 30, 2006

- **Exhortation! for Voice, Piano, and Cello; *It's Not Who Lived Here and Vocalise***

Stark Duo (Darel Stark, violin; Georgine Stark, soprano); *Lutheran Church of Honolulu* – April 28, 2001 (Texts by Charles Bukowski)

- **Guitar Suite No. 1 – *Saggese Guitar Suite (Homage to Paganini)***

Christian Saggese; *The rRed Elephant Café*, Honolulu – September 22, 2007

- **Frenetic Unfolding for Solo Violin**

Darel Stark; *Lutheran Church of Honolulu* – February 12, 2000

- **Metamorphosis No. 3 for Solo Violin – Just Do It**

Darel Stark; Composer's 50th Birthday Party – November 6, 2004

- **Prevalent Ruptured Schisms for Solo Violin**

Darel Stark; *Musician's Union Studio*, Honolulu – August 13, 2010

- **Seeds of Doubt for String Orchestra**

*Moravian Philharmonic Orchestra* – August 13, 2020

- **Japanese Landscape (In Eno's Garden of Possibilities)**

Early piano piece from 1988; Francesco Attesti, pianist; *S. Domenico Church*, Cortona, Italy – August 13, 2015

- **Romantica Passione Suite for Guitar and Violin**

*Romanzo! Splendido Affare* – Hotel Oasi, Cortona, Italy – July 17, 2006
*La Tortura dell'Amore and Un Giorno Teso* – Monti del Parterre Amphitheater, Cortona, Italy – July 21, 2006
Performed by Duo 46

- **Metamorphosis No. 13 for Solo Flute**

Lisa Cella, flutist; *Monti del Parterre Amphitheater,* Cortona, Italy – July 18, 2006

- **Piano Preludes:** *Watery Abstractions, Edward's Polymath,* and *The Emperor's Gestures in His Majestic Garden* played by Hugh Sung, pianist-in-residence at the Curtis Institute of Music; *Cabrini College*, Pennsylvania – November 9, 2005

- **Power Games**

Brent Nitta; *Hawai'i Music Awards Ceremony* – 2006

- **Fanfare for Two Trumpets – 10th Anniversary Honolulu Triathlon Fanfare**

Premiered at the *Honolulu Triathlon* – 2013

- **Piano Suite No. 3**

Nathanael May, piano; *Teatro Signorelli Loggia*, Cortona, Italy – June 24, 2005

## *Multimedia Projects*

- **Anguish in Every Household**

Adapted into a short film featuring an orchestral score paired with evocative 19th-century photographs by Julia Margaret Cameron. The film intensifies the emotional landscape of the music, exploring themes of domestic struggle, grief, and human dignity through a marriage of sound and image.

- **Maxon Crumb Visuals with Hugh Sung**

A multimedia collaboration presented online (*YouTube*, January 3, 2007) featuring Hugh Sung performing *Piano Prelude No. 1*, accompanied by original artwork from my personal collection by Maxon Crumb. The project marries audio and visual art, extending the musical narrative through fine art, and serves as a unique creative bridge between music and illustration.

### *Awards & Recognition*

- **Ampersand**

Winner – 10th Annual *Hawai'i Music Awards* (Classical Music Album), 2006

- **Piano Etude No. II – Sightless**

*Global Music Awards* – Silver Medal for outstanding achievement. Featured on PARMA Recordings' *Pinnacle, Vol. 2*

- **Passing on Ancient Skills for Piano and Orchestra (2024)**

*Global Music Awards* – Silver Medal for outstanding achievement. Featured on PARMA Recordings' *Journey to Serenity*

- **String Quartet No. 3 (Quantum Dice), First Movement (God Does Not Play Dice with the Universe)**

*Global Music Awards* – Silver Medal for outstanding achievement. Featured on PARMA Recordings' *Strung Together*

## Collaborations

- **With Christian Saggese** – Classical guitarist

Collaborations include the *Saggese Guitar Suite* and other recording projects

- **With Andrea Hollander** – Poet

Song cycle settings of selected poems from *Blue Mistaken for Sky* and other works

- **With Darel Stark** – Violinist

Various recording projects for solo violin and ensemble

- **With Nathanael May** – Pianist

Coordinated live concert of solo piano music in Cortona, Italy

- **With Robert Wehrman** – Composer

*Chronicles of a Whipped Creamer for Brass Quintet*, 2009

# SCORE

## XIV
# Piano Etude
## Histories II
## Passing on Ancient Skills

for Hugh Sung

Note: Grace notes are to be played before the beat.

John A. Carollo
(ASCAP)

mf
with increasing forward motion
accel. poco a poco
8vb
8va
8va
8vb
f
mf

sempre
intense
with brilliance
sub. p

36
38
mp
mf
40
marcato
42
ff

marcato

53
8va
55
8va
8vb
p
57
mf
59
mp

61
f
8va
63 (8va)
ff
65
8va
fff
8vb
68
ff
f

Rit.
Delicate
with Beauty
of Tone
(lightly)
come primo
poco rit.
(lighty)
Rit. al fine
come primo

83
ppp
8vb

# ABOUT ATMOSPHERE PRESS

Founded in 2015, Atmosphere Press was built on the principles of Honesty, Transparency, Professionalism, Kindness, and Making Your Book Awesome. As an ethical and author-friendly hybrid press, we stay true to that founding mission today.

If you're a reader, enter our giveaway for a free book here:

SCAN TO ENTER
BOOK GIVEAWAY

If you're a writer, submit your manuscript for consideration here:

SCAN TO SUBMIT
MANUSCRIPT

And always feel free to visit Atmosphere Press and our authors online at atmospherepress.com. See you there soon!

# ABOUT THE AUTHOR

Born in Turin, Italy, in 1954, John A. Carollo was adopted by second-generation Italians and raised in Pennsylvania. A lifelong musician, he sang in a Catholic choir and began composing for piano in 1986. After earning a master's degree in psychology from SDSU, he worked as a mental-health counselor in Honolulu before devoting himself to music full-time. Founder of Musica Baudino, he has released acclaimed recordings including *Ampersand* (2006), *Starry Night* (2011), *The Transfiguration of Giovanni Baudino* (2017), *Music from the Ethereal Side of Paradise* (2018), and *Symphony No. 3* (2019). His work unites lyricism, depth, and emotional clarity.

**For a full list of compositions, please visit www.johncarollocomposer.com.**